WEDDING SHOWERS

WEDDING SHOWERS

IDEAS & RECIPES FOR THE PERFECT PARTY

by michele adams and gia russo   photographs by jonelle weaver

CHRONICLE BOOKS

SAN FRANCISCO

Library of Congress Cataloging-in-Publication Data:

Adams, Michele.
Wedding showers : ideas and recipes for the perfect party / by Michele Adams
and Gia Russo ; photographs by Jonelle Weaver.
p. cm.
ISBN 0-8118-2677-5 (pb)
1. Showers (Parties). 2. Weddings. I. Russo, Gia. II. Title.
GV1472.7.S5A32 2000
793.2—dc21   99-40620
                                                  CIP

Printed in Hong Kong.

Prop styling by Michele Adams and Gia Russo
Food styling by Kimberly Huson
Designed by Sara Schneider

The photographer would like to thank Andy Kitchen for his assistance,
    and Eric Tucker Photography for use of his studio. An additional thanks
    to Kimberly, Mary Beth, and Rhonda for their awesome food styling.

Distributed in Canada by Raincoast Books
8680 Cambie Street
Vancouver, British Columbia V6P 6M9

10 9 8 7 6 5 4 3 2 1

Chronicle Books
85 Second Street
San Francisco, California 94105
www.chroniclebooks.com

DEDICATION

To my husband, John, for his love, support, and constant enthusiasm—I could not have done this without you. To my parents, who taught me to believe that I could accomplish anything. To my grandmother, whose wisdom and sensibility is a great influence on my life.   —Michele

To my husband, Michael, for always being there to love me, support me, and make me laugh. I love you. To my mom, for making me all that I am, and to my Dad, for giving me the courage to reach for my dreams.   —Gia

ACKNOWLEDGMENTS

The creation of this book has involved the help of so many people. From the very moment we decided to take on *Wedding Showers*, the support of our friends and families has been crucial to its success. Our editors, Leslie Jonath and Mikyla Bruder, have been there at every step with careful guidance and encouragement. Jonelle Weaver's keen eye transformed our ideas into beautiful photography, and Kimberly Huson illustrated her incredible culinary talent while working tirelessly on the project.

Many others dedicated time and effort. We thank Stephen Breimer for his sage advice, Amanda Adams for her skilled workmanship, and Jacqueline and John Adams for letting us shoot in their beautiful home. Jackie Mallos and Julie Auerbach generously gave their time to grace the pages of this book, and Richard Volker was quick to lend a hand to support the crew. Eric Tucker kindly allowed us to use his studio, and Kamal Sandhu graciously loaned us furniture and accessories from her shop, Shelter, in Los Angeles.

INTRODUCTION

Wedding showers are about friends and family coming together to enjoy great food in a beautiful setting, and honoring the bride-to-be with gifts and memories to last a lifetime. There is no better way to honor the engaged couple than with an intimate and personal shower. And for the host, the shower is an opportunity to create a wonderful memory for the bride (or couple) that will accompany her into married life.

The shower, while considered an American tradition, is culled from celebrations found in cultures around the world. For example, ancient Egyptians celebrated a union by inviting friends and relatives to a banquet hall decorated with flowers and lights. The groom did his part by presenting the bride with a gift of jewelry. In Holland, families once decorated evergreen-covered thrones for the bride and groom to sit on while guests extended good wishes. Today, relatives of the Chinese bride and groom offer pocketbooks filled with precious gold jewelry. And the Iraqi groom raises money for gifts that he presents to his bride and her family.

It's not certain when or where the first shower was given. In the earliest records, marriage was a complicated process involving lengthy contracts and an exchange of property. This property, the dowry, was made up of household goods such as linens, clothing, kitchen equipment, and, more important, a lump sum of money that was presented to the groom in trust since women were not allowed to inherit money or property. The exchange was meant to ensure the bride's financial stability and social status in her married life.

A turning point in this tradition occurred in medieval Amsterdam. As with all marriages during that time, the bride's family was required to provide a dowry. One young woman in Amsterdam found herself unable to marry when her father objected to her chosen groom, thus refusing her dowry. Because the bride was well liked in her village, many of the townspeople joined together, bringing linens, household goods, and tableware—and so making a dowry for the grateful bride.

Throughout the eighteenth century, the conventions of the dowry evolved as women took a more active role in preparing for their marriages. The French equivalent of the dowry, the *trousseau*, contained household necessities a young woman collected or made herself—and bundled together into a neat package (*trousseau* means, literally, "bundle") to take to her married home. Delicate embroidery and intricate woodwork carvings embellished ordinary linens and tableware.

In America our dowry is the hope chest, the popularity of which corresponded with a revival in romanticism during the Victorian period of the mid- to late 1800s. Women of this time took pride in storing their precious household goods in a sturdy trunk that would be taken with them to their new home. These hope chests (referring to the wishes made by young women dreaming about being in love) were crafted from the finest hardwoods and often handed down from generation to generation. It was also during this time that the first modern showers were hosted. Typically formal afternoon teas or luncheons, these women-only parties gave the bride a chance to display some of the treasures from her hope chest and for guests to give special gifts to include in the chest.

Here in the United States, it has long been customary for the maid of honor or a brides-maid to throw the wedding shower, and for women friends and women family members to come bearing gifts and good wishes. Today, it is just as common for men to make the guest list, and for either the bride or groom's family to host the shower. Solemn traditions of years past are being reinterpreted in favor of throwing a party that truly honors the charac-ter and individuality of the bride or couple. But however the traditions are interpreted, the spirit of the wedding shower remains one of celebration and generosity—an honoring of the meeting of lives. If you are chosen to throw a shower for a loved one, you will no doubt want to plan a thoughtful and fitting tribute to this momentous occasion. *Wedding Showers* is meant to give you a starting point in this endeavor.

In dreaming up ideas for this book, both of us were amazed at how many ideas we had accumulated. In our years working as editors and stylists for *Martha Stewart Living*, we used our experiences to develop our own style of entertaining. In writing this book, we adapted ideas from the many showers we hosted and attended. Our "Afternoon of Desserts" is inspired by Gia's shower, an intimate tea party hosted by her friend Helen Quinn. The handmade invitations featured dress silhouettes cut from handkerchief linen and glued to the front of the cards. Helen prepared delicate tea sandwiches and cookies and served them on her grandmother's silver trays. Beautifully wrapped gifts were adorned with silk ribbons, fresh flowers, and small accessories, such as wooden spoons, that hinted at the gifts inside. The shower was a great success, and we both noticed how many people there asked for advice about how to host a wedding shower.

By coincidence we moved to the West Coast within a month of one another and decided to collaborate on projects where we could use all the wonderful ideas we had collected over the years—ideas that express our own personal style. This book is one of those projects. With little out there on the subject that isn't sadly outdated, we wanted to create a book that was truly useful. No more cookie-cutter showers for women with the same old games, fussy decorations, and stuffy rules. Showers today, like people, are much more relaxed, and we wanted our book to offer practical and creative ideas for throwing unique, personalized showers.

In *Wedding Showers,* we present four showers that can be adapted to any situation. You will find a range of styles—from an updated version of an elegant, traditional shower to a coed beach barbecue—and a range of menus, decorations, and locations that can be tailored to fit your needs. We have found that the most successful showers have a theme that reflects the spirit of the bride or the couple. Themes set the mood, determine the guest list, influence the menu, suggest gifts, and above all, bring focus to the guest (or guests) of honor.
No matter what the theme or style, showers are a wonderful way to celebrate a great milestone in life. Like any party, there is running around to be done and decisions to be made. What type of food would you like to serve? Where should it take place? How should it look? And like most busy people, we know it is important to get the party together quickly and inexpensively. But there is no better way to make someone feel special than to put real thought and energy into creating a party just for them. We hope the ideas in this book will inspire and help you to host memorable showers for the people you love.

1 2 3 4 5

THE WEDDING SHOWER

Once you have offered to host a wedding shower, you will need to do some preliminary brainstorming. It's important to discuss the shower with the bride or engaged couple, keeping in mind that this celebration should reflect their wishes and desires. There are a variety of issues to consider—their preference for a coed or traditional guest list, possible themes and how they might relate to the season. The practical items to review include when and where the party will take place and how the location might be affected by the weather. Then you're ready to tackle some of the finer points—invitations, decorations, menu, favors, gifts, and how to prepare and organize it all.

Determining the number of guests to invite to a wedding shower will depend on many factors—the number of showers being hosted for the couple, the size of their wedding guest list, and the number of friends and family in the area where the shower will take place. Before deciding exactly who to invite, keep in mind its intimate nature—a shower shouldn't overshadow the more important wedding ceremony and reception. Because the couple is likely to have many different circles of friends, relatives, and coworkers, it's possible that more than one person would want to host showers for them. Therefore, some guests might be invited to only one shower, while some will be invited to several. Generally, etiquette dictates inviting only guests who are also invited to the wedding. The exceptions would be an office shower hosted by coworkers, or a situation in which the couple is opting for a small or destination wedding. Consult the bride when making the decision about the guest list; she will surely be able to help you decide who to invite.

Once you know how many guests you will need to accommodate, consider where the party will take place. You needn't limit yourself to the obvious. If the weather is good, a garden, terrace, or even park or beach would make an excellent location for a large gathering. Your home or garden may be the ideal place. You have constant access to it, and no limit to the amount of time you can take for preparation. Look at your home with a renewed purpose, and you will find many possibilities. A dining room or even a hallway can be cleared of furniture to accommodate a buffet table. If possible, remove extra furniture and accessories from the room you'll be using—that way your party-decorating efforts won't compete with the surroundings. Whether you've decided to have the shower indoors or out, the fact that there will be people coming to your house will most likely spur you into action. It's not the time to take on a huge remodeling project—simply focus on cleaning the areas where guests will be. Don't forget the bathroom. A stack of clean hand towels, fresh soaps, and an extra roll of toilet paper will be appreciated. Tidy up the garden and entry area, repotting containers with blooming plants if necessary.

The invitation itself should hint at the theme and mood of the party, and guests will react with greater anticipation to one that's thoughtfully designed. Invitations should go out three to four weeks in advance and should feature an RSVP date and a phone number. Your RSVP date should give guests enough notice to respond to the invitation (a minimum of seven days will suffice, but two weeks is better) and still allow the host time to make any last-minute adjustments. Be sure to factor in enough time up front for gathering the address list, making and addressing the invitations, and a few days for delivery. For a smaller shower like the "Day of Beauty," a simple phone call to each guest may suffice, but you should still give guests plenty of advance notice.

It's a good idea to browse in your local art or paper store, where you'll find most of the supplies needed to make any invitation: textured watercolor paper, translucent vellum (available in prints and pastels), and precut cardstock (available in a huge variety of colors these days). Wallpapers come in unusual colors and patterns and can be glued to a piece of cardstock (so it won't curl up) and used as background for a smaller printed card, leaving a beautiful border around the invitation. Keep in mind that not all papers will work for every method of printing, so choose accordingly.

Handmade cards don't need to be complicated. A piece of sheer vellum tied with a snippet of satin ribbon to a crisp cardstock paper assembles quickly and makes a beautiful invitation. Experiment with different inks, stamps, or craft cutouts in different shapes and motifs. The addition of a small detail—a tiny piece of fabric trimming glued along the edges—can transform a simple card into a true standout.

THE MENU

Planning a menu that tastes great, looks beautiful, and is easy to prepare may seem like a tall order, but the four menus on these pages really meet each of those requirements. Since each shower is designed around a theme, menus are chosen to complement the setting and mood. The "Beach Barbecue" focuses on prepare-ahead hearty foods that will hold up throughout the day, while the fresh and light "Day of Beauty" menu complements the spa theme. Although we developed each menu for a general number of people, they can be tailored to fit your needs and adjusted to the size and season of the shower.

Since preparing the food is perhaps one of the most time consuming tasks of entertaining, we've selected recipes that are easy to prepare. Many can even be made in advance. Consider asking a friend or two to help with the preparation. Michele recently cohosted a shower for which the recipes were divided among four people. Delegating some of the cooking will take a bit of the pressure off of you, and your friends may appreciate being included. Each chapter comes with a section we call "Putting It Together," which will help you manage your time and keep the process smooth and trouble free.

THE AMBIANCE

This is the fun part. What better chance to show off your creative talents than with a beautifully decorated party. Start with an idea that inspires you and take it from there. The showers on these pages began in different ways. Sometimes the inspiration started with ideas about the menu. Cocktails and hors d'oeuvres from Asia and the tropics, for example, defined the look of the setting—green and lush surroundings, and tables brimming with the textures of colorful fruits, rich woods, and bamboo.

The style and mood of any party is affected by a number of factors. Basic choices of color, materials, serving pieces, and food contribute to the end result. The personality of both the host and guest of honor, formality of the party, and location should all be considered during the initial planning stages. Color is one of the simplest ways to evoke a mood, and we suggest developing a party palette early on. Experiment with colors normally overlooked for a shower. The whimsical and untraditional pairing of hot pink and bright orange in the "Beach Barbecue" evokes cheerfulness and is appropriate for a lighthearted coed outdoor party. The pink and taupe combination in the "Afternoon of Desserts" has a sweet but sophisticated feel. A pure bridal white can be used with any theme for a crisp and clean look.

One thing to remember is that the party doesn't need to be expensive to be a success. You can find all the components for the parties in this book at your local discount craft and import stores. Sheer pale pink tulle is very inexpensive, and draped across a room can instantly transform the setting. A simple arrangement of tropical fruits from the grocery store or farmers' market gives a table an abundant look. No matter what kind of party you choose to throw, the unique details will create the ambiance and leave a lasting impression.

THE FAVORS

Party favors are a great way to thank your guests and leave them with a wonderful remembrance of the shower. There are as many types of favors as there are ways to present them, and dreaming up ideas and even making them yourself is half the fun. For the "Afternoon of Desserts," we filled round chipwood boxes with crinkled tissue strips and Icebox Cookies. A tray near the door offered tidy rows of these favors for guests to take as they said goodbye. Guests of the "Tropical Cocktails" shower chose from the orchid boutonnieres set atop a leaf-covered tray and pinned them to their clothing as they entered the party. Other favors are integral to the theme, providing guests with things they will need at the shower.

For "Beach Barbecue," we painted inexpensive metal buckets bright orange and filled them with dime-store goodies, sunscreen, and snacks. The pails could then be used for building sandcastles, collecting rocks, and toting home the day's finds. Whatever you choose, favors should be individually packaged, portable, and in keeping with the theme of the shower. Small treats like chocolates, cookies, nuts, and candies are inexpensive and easy to package in little boxes and bags. Finished with ribbon, sprigs of leaves, or fresh flowers, the favors become special decorations for the shower, as well as gifts for the guests.

THE GIFTS

In addition to socializing and eating, the primary activity of the shower is the opening of the gifts. It's a chance for the gift-givers to make their special contribution to the couple's life, and the rare opportunity to see their gift opened with ceremony. For the bride or couple, it's a chance to thank each person individually and acknowledge their gifts graciously. We have always been inspired by handmade gifts and think they are especially appropriate for a shower. Whether you make the gift yourself or customize a store-bought gift with details or beautiful packaging, the message you send is caring and thoughtful, sure to be remembered and appreciated.

A good way to start thinking about which gift to give is to check the couple's registry. They have probably selected many items they'll need to start their new home. A set of linen sheets, towels, and robes can be customized with monograms—sew them yourself or have them done professionally. Even ordinary household items like storage baskets, pillows, and laundry bags can be easily transformed into a cherished gift. In the "Afternoon of

Desserts" chapter, we offer a simple craft recipe for a Fabric-lined Basket. We gave one of these baskets to a friend of ours, filling it with rolled towels tied with satin ribbons. Another bride received a galvanized bucket filled with tools and supplies for her garden.

Many people throw showers with gift themes. Some stock the linen closet, while others fill the kitchen with top-quality pots and pans. Consider the interests of the bride and groom. If they are wine lovers, contribute to their wine cellar. If they are campers, explore sporting goods stores for outdoorsy gifts.

No matter what gifts you choose, spend some time making the package beautiful. Simple wrapping is always elegant and easy to pull off successfully. Solid-colored or subtle and simple patterned papers and tissue are a good start. We like translucent papers such as vellum, which comes in many colors and can be fashioned into a cuff that wraps around the package, giving it a two-toned look. Ribbons in satin, velvet, grosgrain, and silk, as well as other delicate trimmings, are an easy way to make a package look extraordinary. Experiment with different proportions and colors—try skinny velvet ribbons in multiples across a long package, or a wide ribbon around a small package. Fresh and silk flowers can be tied into the bow for a quick and beautiful embellishment.

GETTING ORGANIZED

Hosting any party will give even the most organized person some anxiety, but you can avoid some of that by starting early with a good plan. Here are some tips that will help you maintain a sense of control over the planning process and alleviate stress before and during the shower. Our "Party Planner" (page 21) is meant as a general outline for getting organized. Each chapter begins with specific advice on putting together the party.

Once you've made all the practical decisions about the guest list, invitations, location, menu, decorations, favors, and gifts, you'll need to figure out what is needed and how to plan the work. It's never too early to start organizing and planning and there are plenty of things to do even at the earliest stages. We like to make a master list of everything we need to accomplish and then organize that list into a time schedule, which keeps us from pushing everything to the last minute. The master list is also a good place to make shopping lists. Organize your shopping lists by the type of store you're going to patronize: grocery, crafts, fabric, hardware. It's a good idea to make your shopping lists right away and keep them with you in case you have a free moment to do a quick errand. You want to prevent wasting valuable time making extra trips to the store, especially during the critical few days before the shower. Just remember, the more you can put down on paper the more in control you'll feel, and the less likely you'll be to forget things.

One or two weeks before the shower, set aside some time to clean and organize around the house or yard—this will free your time for last-minute preparations. Gather together and set aside the household materials you'll be using for the party. Michele learned a great entertaining trick from her mother: make a list of everything you'll need from your collection of linens, serving pieces, tableware, and accessories. Wash and iron the linens, if necessary, and set them aside where they won't be disturbed. Wash and polish serving pieces like platters, vases for flower arrangements, candleholders, plates, and silverware.

Do a practice setting of the table or buffet to confirm that your choices work together. This gives you a chance to make any changes in your plan, or to note any items that you will need.

You should shop for decorating items, and shop for or make your gift to the bride, at least a few weeks in advance. Spend some time wrapping and decorating the package, and you won't have to worry about it again. If your favors can be made ahead, get those out of the way as well. With those details taken care of, you will be free to concentrate on the decorations and food preparation that will occupy you in the few days before the shower. The menus in this book are designed with many recipes that can be prepared ahead of time. Shopping can be grouped into three lists: kitchen and baking supplies, groceries for the week before, and groceries for a day or two before the shower. In the early stages, scan each recipe to note how far in advance it can be made. Create a food preparation schedule, noting what to make on which day. If you plan to enlist the help of friends or relatives, coordinate this schedule with them. You will find more specific menu preparation information for each shower in the following chapters.

The most important thing to remember is that throwing a party is supposed to be fun. Making the lists and creating the schedules may seem like more work, but you will appreciate it in the end. The more organizing you do up front, the more enjoyable the process will be. And remember, it is a general rule that if the host is having fun, chances are the guests will have fun too. So plan rigorously, and enjoy the party.

This quick guideline will give you a general sense of how to organize your time before the party. Feel free to adapt it to fit your own schedule.

SIX OR MORE WEEKS AHEAD
Speak with bride about basic decisions of date, location, time of day, guest list, theme, and style of shower
Make master "to do" planning list

FOUR TO SIX WEEKS AHEAD
Gather address list of guests
Shop for or make invitations and shower gift
Choose menu
Place order for any rental equipment

THREE TO FOUR WEEKS AHEAD
Shop for decorations and any special serving pieces or supplies
Send out invitations
Work on special decorations like tablecloths and favors

TWO TO THREE WEEKS AHEAD
Gather and clean serving pieces, table linens, and tableware
Make shopping lists for recipe ingredients
Place flower order

ONE TO TWO WEEKS AHEAD
Wrap shower gift
Begin cleaning house and/or yard

FIVE TO SEVEN DAYS AHEAD
Shop for recipe ingredients
Begin setting up for party
Confirm order and/or delivery time for rentals and flowers
Finish any last-minute decorations
Finish cleaning party location
Confirm RSVPs

1 (2) 3 4 5

AN AFTERNOON OF DESSERTS

DECORATIONS AND FAVORS

ROSE BALL

EASY FABRIC SWAG

SHEER TABLE RUNNER

SIMPLE SILK NAPKINS

FABRIC-LINED BASKET

COOKIE BOX FAVORS

MENU

ICEBOX COOKIES

HANDMADE TRUFFLES

SHORTBREAD WEDGES WITH PIPED CHOCOLATE

COCONUT LEMON LAYER CAKE

BERRY BREAD PUDDINGS

DOUBLE CHOCOLATE RASPBERRY CAKE

POUND CAKE SQUARES WITH MIXED BERRIES

CHOCOLATE MOUSSE WITH RASPBERRIES

PRETTY PETAL PUNCH

COFFEE AND TEA

*P*erfect for a bride who wants a traditional shower, this afternoon tea showcases a beautiful assortment of irresistible desserts. Inspired by the lavish afternoon teas popular during the Victorian period, this party updates tradition with a modern approach, featuring coffee, tea, punch, and delectable desserts displayed elegantly on a buffet table. Icebox Cookies placed in small boxes lined with shredded paper and tied with satin ribbons make a great party favor, leaving guests with a sweet memory of the party. This is a good shower to hold in your home; any number of spaces, indoors and out, will accommodate the dessert buffet. The simple decorations will transform any space and can be put up ahead of time.

The menu is designed for a party of twenty guests, but it can easily be varied according to your needs. Serve fewer items for a smaller crowd, eliminating a recipe or two. For a larger crowd, plan to make two or even three of each recipe. The Chocolate Mousse with Raspberries, Berry Bread Puddings, Double Chocolate Raspberry Cake, and Pound Cake Squares with Mixed Berries feature berries available in the summer months, but all of these recipes can be prepared with the fruits of the season.

For the soft but sophisticated ambiance, we chose a feminine pale pink as the primary color. Pink has long been associated with brides and weddings, and its combination with a creamy taupe feels modern while retaining a delicate quality. We customized invitations printed on pale pink by attaching a tiny pink embroidered flower appliqué to the top of each card. The embroidered flower echoes the traditional gift theme of linens, and hints at the mood of the party.

In setting up for the party, we rearranged the furniture in the dining room to make space for the dessert buffet. The table is set back and framed by French doors draped with yards of inexpensive pink tulle. Extra tulle adorns the entry hall and the living room where the gifts would be opened. The Rose Ball, a lovely decoration of pink and taupe roses, hangs from a length of wide satin ribbon in the middle of the swag. Pink rose petals add color to the buffet, floating atop the Pretty Petal Punch and scattered throughout the desserts. A variety of pale pink fabrics cover the tables. We used a soft cotton for the base tablecloth, beautifully showing off the Sheer Table Runner made with silk organza bordered with taupe satin ribbon. The Simple Silk Napkins are made with leftover silk organza literally ripped into squares.

Linen is a traditional theme for shower gifts, and the Fabric-lined Basket is a thoughtful way to present your gift. Lined with a loose weave of cotton fabric, the basket can be filled with a gift of linens. Keep in mind, if you intend to make a handmade gift, you'll want to work that into your party plan, at least a few weeks before the shower.

In setting up your buffet, take advantage of the variety of shapes, sizes, and tastes—sweet, tart, rich, and light—featured in these desserts. We chose the desserts for their unique colors, textures, sizes, or shapes. Each dessert is best arranged next to others with contrasting features. Place the Coconut Lemon Layer Cake next to the Handmade Truffles, the Chocolate Mousse with Raspberries next to the rustic Berry Bread Puddings. When setting the buffet, don't forget to leave room for a stack of dessert plates, napkins, and silverware at one end. Punch and cups are easier to handle at the other end of the buffet. Coffee and tea are the last to prepare. Set them out just a few minutes before guests begin to arrive so they are piping hot and ready to serve.

TWO WEEKS AHEAD
- Make the Sheer Table Runner and Simple Silk Napkins
- Order roses from florist

FOUR DAYS AHEAD
- Make Icebox Cookies and finish assembling favors
- Hang Easy Fabric Swag

TWO DAYS AHEAD
- Set out table linens, touching up with iron if needed
- Set out serving pieces, plates, silverware, napkins, punch bowl and cups, and favor boxes
- Make Shortbread dough and Handmade Truffles
- Bake Pound Cake Squares
- Pick up roses for Rose Ball and buffet

THE DAY BEFORE
- Receive and set up rentals
- Shop for last-minute recipe ingredients
- Bake Shortbread Wedges, Coconut Lemon Layer Cake, Double Chocolate Raspberry Cake, and Berry Bread Puddings
- Make Chocolate Mousse

THE MORNING OF THE SHOWER
- Assemble Rose Ball and hang in place
- Drizzle chocolate over Shortbread Wedges
- Make frostings and decorate cakes

A FEW HOURS BEFORE
- Spoon Chocolate Mousse into glass goblets
- Assemble Pound Cake Squares with Mixed Berries
- Decorate buffet with rose petals

JUST BEFORE THE SHOWER
- Set out desserts on buffet and arrange garnish
- Make Pretty Petal Punch and add ice to punch bowl
- Make coffee and tea

ROSE BALL

You can use any roses you like for this decoration—we prefer the 'Bridal Pink' and 'Sahara' varieties. You should purchase the roses a day or two ahead of the party to give the blooms time to open. Assemble the ball on the morning of the shower—it's easier if you can get a friend to help hold the ball while you work. Once made, the Rose Ball will last for 8 to 12 hours.

For each Rose Ball you will need:

4 TO 5 DOZEN PINK AND TAUPE ROSES (DEPENDING ON THE SIZE OF THE ROSE)

24 INCHES OF 1^1/$_2$-INCH PINK RIBBON

ONE 8-INCH STYROFOAM BALL

5 T-PINS (FOUND IN THE NOTIONS SECTION AT FABRIC OR DISCOUNT STORES)

GLUE GUN (AND GLUE STICKS)

CUP HOOK

Purchase the roses a day or two ahead of the party. When you get them home, remove thorns and leaves and cut stems on an angle at least 1 inch from the bottom. Place roses in buckets of cool water and keep in a cool place until the morning of the shower. To get blooms to open quickly, recut stems at an angle at least 1 inch from the bottom and place in buckets filled with very warm water.

Place the center of the ribbon on the ball and use the T-pins to secure the ribbon. This will be the top center of the Rose Ball. Add a touch of glue for extra hold. Allow to dry.

Cut the rose heads off the stems, making sure the bottom of each head is flat. Using the glue gun, place four drops of glue on the back of each rose. Place the roses on the ball, allowing each to dry a few minutes before moving on. As you progress, find a place to hang the ball in order to avoid crushing the roses. Let the finished ball dry for 30 minutes before hanging it from a cup hook in its final location.

EASY FABRIC SWAG

A fabric swag made of tulle or chiffon is an easy and inexpensive way to transform a room. In this case, we draped the fabric around a set of French doors, but windows, or even plain walls, are great candidates for swath of color.

For each Easy Fabric Swag you will need:

TAPE MEASURE

CUP HOOKS

SHEER FABRIC SUCH AS TULLE OR
    CHIFFON

Once you've decided on the framework, measure the dimensions (length, height, and width) of the walls and ceiling space that will be covered in fabric, and add some extra to allow the fabric to swag. We used 18 yards of pale pink tulle to drape over an 8-foot-high-by-8-foot-wide set of doors (fabric was doubled up to create a fuller look).

Screw cup hooks into place at the two upper corners and at the center-point of the space. Hang the fabric along the length of the space, bunching the fabric into the cup hooks and allowing it to drape gracefully between each hook. If desired, hang a Rose Ball (page 29) from the center cup hook.

The runner is sized for a 72-by-30-inch table. See the note below for instructions for altering the measurements to fit a different-sized table. Before using the finished runner, cover your table with a basic cotton tablecloth to form a base. The napkins are deceptively simple to make, and they are a great finish to your buffet table.

For each Sheer Table Runner and 20 Simple Silk Napkins you will need:

TAPE MEASURE

4 YARDS PALE PINK SHEER ORGANDY
    FABRIC, 48 INCHES WIDE

IRON

SCISSORS

7 1/2 YARDS 3-INCH TAUPE SATIN
    RIBBON

SEWING MACHINE

To make the runner, measure and rip the fabric into a 36-inch-wide piece. Fold in half lengthwise, matching the torn edges, to make an 18-inch-wide strip. Press the folded edge with a warm iron. Fold and press the torn edges under 1/2 inch. Fold and press under another 1/2 inch.

Measure and cut four pieces of ribbon, one for each side of the runner, leaving about 4 inches of excess on each side. Stitch the ribbon to the runner along each edge finishing corners by overlapping the ribbons where they intersect, folding the ends of ribbons under, and stitching down the edges in a square.

To make the napkins, measure 9-inch increments along a machined edge of the fabric, and cut about half an inch into the fabric at each increment. At each side of the cut, grip fabric tightly and rip through. You will end up with four 9-inch-wide strips of fabric. Measure 9-inch sections along the length of these strips, then cut and rip fabric as before to make twenty 9-by-9-inch squares. If desired, create frayed edges by pulling threads out until the fray is about 1/2 inch wide. Press napkins with a warm iron.

Note: To tailor the project to fit a different-sized table, measure the width of your table and subtract 8 inches. This allows for 4 inches of table space on either side of the runner. Now measure the length of your table and add 18 inches (enough for the runner to hang over each end of the table).

FABRIC-LINED BASKET

Search craft or houseware stores for a pretty basket and line it with two crisscrossing lengths of colorful fabric. We used a rectangular basket with handles, but a square basket will work just fine, too. Stuff the lined basket with rolled towels and clothespins, a stack of crisp embroidered linens, or a pair of fluffy down pillows tied with wide satin ribbon. No wrapping necessary!

For each Fabric-lined Basket you will need:

RECTANGULAR WICKER BASKET

TAPE MEASURE

COTTON FABRIC

SCISSORS

IRON

SEWING MACHINE

NEEDLE AND HEAVY THREAD

The simple fabric lining is composed of 2 lengths of fabric crisscrossing at the bottom of the basket. To determine the dimensions of the longer fabric piece, measure the inside of the basket starting at the top of one narrow side, down the side, across the bottom, and up the opposite side. Add 12 inches to this measurement (10 inches to allow the fabric to hang over the sides of the basket plus 1 inch for seam allowance). Measure across the bottom width (perpendicular to your first measurement) of the basket and add 1 inch for seam allowance. Cut 1 fabric piece to these dimensions.

To determine the dimensions of the shorter fabric piece, measure the inside of the basket starting at the top of one wider side, down the side, across the bottom, and up the opposite side. Add 1 inch to this measurement for seam allowance. Measure across the bottom width of the basket and add 1 inch for seam allowance. Cut 1 fabric piece to these dimensions.

Using an iron, fold and press under 1/4 inch along the edges of each fabric piece. Fold and press under another 1/4 inch. Machine stitch the edges close to the fold, or hand stitch along the fold. Fit the two pieces of fabric into the basket. The ends of the longer piece sould hang over the two narrow sides of the basket, and the shorter piece of fabric should overlap the longer along the bottom. Using the needle and thread, stitch the edges of the fabric to the wicker, securing the lining to the basket.

These little treats are simple to put together and can be prepared up to five days in advance of the party. Make one for each of your guests. Accordion-fold shredded paper and small wooden boxes are available at good craft stores.

For each Cookie Box Favor you will need:

WHITE ACCORDION-FOLD SHREDDED
    PAPER

3-INCH-DIAMETER ROUND WOOD BOX

ICEBOX COOKIE (PAGE 36)

1/4-INCH PINK PICOT RIBBON, 12
    INCHES LONG

Place the shredded paper in the bottom of the box. Place the cookie on top of the paper and cover with the lid. Tie the ribbon around the box like a package and finish off with a knot.

34

ICEBOX COOKIES

Our food stylist, Kimberly Huson, gave us her grandmother's recipe for these light and delicious cookies. They can be made ahead (up to five days in advance); package in miniature wooden boxes tied with ribbon as favors for your guests.

2 CUPS ALL-PURPOSE FLOUR

2 TEASPOONS BAKING POWDER

$1/2$ TEASPOON SALT

$1/2$ CUP UNSALTED BUTTER

1 CUP LIGHT BROWN SUGAR

1 EGG

1 TEASPOON VANILLA

1 CUP WALNUTS, CHOPPED

Sift together the flour, baking powder, and salt in a medium bowl and set aside. In a separate bowl, cream the butter and sugar until well blended. Add the egg and vanilla, then beat until light and fluffy. Add the flour mixture a half cup at a time, mixing well after each addition. Add the walnuts and mix to incorporate. Place the dough on a clean board and roll into a log approximately $2 1/2$ inches in diameter. Wrap the dough log in waxed paper, fold ends under or tie with kitchen string to seal, and chill for at least 2 hours and up to 5 days.

When you are ready to bake the cookies, preheat oven to 350° F. Unwrap dough log and slice crosswise into thin rounds approximately $1/4$ inch thick. Bake on a cookie sheet lightly coated with nonstick spray for approximately 8 minutes.

Makes about 3 dozen.

A good-quality chocolate is the key to a smooth, creamy truffle. Using this basic recipe, truffles can be decorated with a variety of ingredients—dusted with unsweetened cocoa powder, drizzled with chocolate, or rolled in nuts. Truffles can be made a few days in advance, or if you're short on time, a good confectionery shop is a great source for ready-made truffles.

10 OUNCES GOOD-QUALITY
BITTERSWEET CHOCOLATE

$1/2$ CUP HEAVY CREAM

4 TABLESPOONS UNSALTED BUTTER
AT ROOM TEMPERATURE

$1/2$ CUP UNSWEETENED COCOA
POWDER

Using a serrated knife, chop the chocolate into small, evenly sized pieces and place in a medium-size metal bowl. In a small saucepan, heat the cream over medium heat just until it starts to bubble. Remove from heat immediately and allow to cool less than a minute. Pour the cream, all at once, over the chocolate and stir with a rubber spatula until the mixture is completely incorporated. While the chocolate mixture is still warm, add the butter and stir until completely smooth, forming a ganache. Keeping ganache in the bowl, cover loosely with plastic and chill in refrigerator until just cool but not firm.

Pour ganache into a pastry bag fitted with a $1/2$-inch tip, and line a few baking sheets with wax paper. Holding pastry bag vertical, pipe 1-inch-diameter dollops onto baking sheet. Chill in refrigerator until firm, about 1 hour.

Place the cocoa powder or other toppings, such as chopped nuts, in separate shallow dishes and remove truffles from refrigerator. Roll each truffle between your hands to smooth and heat slightly to allow topping to adhere easily. Roll truffle in the topping, and carefully place in a waxed paper candy cup. Store covered at room temperature.

Makes approximately 60 truffles.

SHORTBREAD WEDGES WITH PIPED CHOCOLATE

We've updated this traditional recipe with melted chocolate drizzled over the shortbread, adding richness and texture. The dough can be made up to two days in advance and refrigerated until ready to bake.

1 CUP ALL-PURPOSE FLOUR

$1/2$ CUP CORNSTARCH

$3/4$ CUP POWDERED SUGAR

$3/4$ TEASPOON SALT

$1/2$ CUP UNSALTED COLD BUTTER,
CUT INTO PIECES

2 TABLESPOONS COLD MILK

6 OUNCES SEMISWEET CHOCOLATE,
CHOPPED, OR CHOCOLATE CHIPS

Place the flour, cornstarch, sugar, and salt in a food processor. Pulse several times to blend. Add the butter pieces, one at a time, and pulse until the mixture resembles a coarse meal. Add the milk, 1 tablespoon at a time, and pulse until mixture holds together to form a ball; press flat. Wrap in plastic and refrigerate for $1/2$ hour or up to 2 days.

Preheat oven to 375° F. Using fingers, press dough evenly into an 8-inch round or square pan. Bake at 375° F for 10 minutes, then reduce temperature to 325° F and bake for an additional 30 minutes. Remove from oven and allow to cool slightly. Working carefully, turn pan over onto cutting board. Using a sharp knife, cut shortbread into triangles or squares while still slightly warm and allow to cool in place.

To decorate, transfer the shortbread to baking racks positioned over sheets of waxed paper. Place the chocolate in a microwave-safe bowl. Heat chocolate in microwave for 1 minute and stir with a plastic spatula. Continue heating chocolate in microwave for 20-second intervals, stirring each time until chocolate is completely melted. Pour melted chocolate into a plastic squirt bottle or resealable bag. If using the plastic bag, snip off a very small piece of the corner to allow chocolate to drizzle out. Squeeze the melted chocolate over cooled shortbread using a circular motion in a swirling pattern. Place the shortbread in a cool place to allow chocolate to set before storing in a plastic container.

Makes about 12 wedges.

COCONUT LEMON LAYER CAKE

Shredded coconut gives this lemon-infused cake extra sweetness and a fluffy white look. We suggest baking
the cake the night before and frosting it a few hours before the shower.

1 BOX LEMON CAKE MIX

ONE 3¹/2-OUNCE BOX LEMON
   PUDDING MIX

¹/4 CUP LEMON JUICE, FRESHLY
   SQUEEZED

¹/4 CUP VEGETABLE OIL

3 EGGS

1 RECIPE LEMON BUTTER FROSTING
   (RECIPE FOLLOWS)

ONE 11¹/4-OUNCE JAR LEMON CURD
   (YOU WON'T USE ALL OF IT)

2 CUPS SHREDDED COCONUT
   (PACKAGED)

Preheat oven to 350° F. Prepare two 8-inch round cake pans with cooking spray. In a large mixing bowl, combine the cake mix, pudding mix, lemon juice, oil, and eggs and beat with an electric mixer for 2 minutes. Pour the batter into cake pans, dividing evenly. Bake for approximately 30 minutes, or until a cake tester or toothpick comes out clean when placed into the center of the cake. Remove from oven and allow to cool on baking racks. Carefully remove cakes from baking pans onto a large cutting board or work surface. Using a serrated knife, slice the round top off each cake, then slice each layer in half horizontally making four layers. Separate each layer and use a soft pastry brush to remove excess crumbs.

Place a cake layer on an inverted cake pan covered with wax paper. Using an offset spatula, spread a thin layer of Lemon Butter Frosting followed by a thin layer of lemon curd on top of the cake. Repeat the process, stacking another cake layer, followed by a layer of frosting and lemon curd, leaving the final, top layer unfinished. With the spatula, frost the sides of the cake evenly and smoothly and continue covering the top. Sprinkle the coconut over the top and using your hands, gently press shreds into the sides of the cake. Transfer the cake to a serving platter or pedestal stand using one or two large spatulas.

Serves 10 to 12.

LEMON BUTTER FROSTING

This lemony frosting can be made up to two days in advance. Cover tightly and store
in the refrigerator until ready to use.

1/2 CUP UNSALTED BUTTER AT ROOM
    TEMPERATURE

3 CUPS POWDERED SUGAR

2 TABLFSPOONS HEAVY CREAM

1 TABLESPOON LEMON JUICE, FRESHLY
    SQUEEZED

1 TEASPOON LEMON ZEST, GRATED

Cream the butter with an electric mixer, in a medium bowl. Add the remaining ingredients and continue mixing until frosting is well blended and fluffy.

Berry bread puddings can be made out of any kind of leftover breads—we like brioche, challah, French, sourdough, and cinnamon. The texture is best if the bread you use is a day old. This recipe is designed for individual servings, but you can make it in a large baking dish too. If you're pressed for time on the day of the shower, you can make this the day before.

---

8 CUPS BREAD, CUBED OR TORN INTO 1½-INCH PIECES

4 CUPS MIXED BERRIES, SUCH AS BLACKBERRY, RASPBERRY, STRAW-BERRY, OR BLUEBERRY (IN ANY COMBINATION)

8 EGGS

1½ CUPS SUGAR

3 CUPS HALF AND HALF

1 TABLESPOON VANILLA

1 TEASPOON CINNAMON

¼ TEASPOON NUTMEG

POWDERED SUGAR FOR DUSTING

Preheat oven to 375° F. Prepare eight individual soufflé cups (1-cup capacity) with cooking spray. In a large bowl, toss the bread cubes with the berries to distribute evenly. In another large bowl, beat the eggs with a whisk or electric mixer on low speed until frothy. Add the sugar and beat until well blended. Add half and half, vanilla, cinnamon, and nut-meg and continue beating on low speed until well blended. Fill soufflé cups with the bread and berry mixture, mounding it a bit on top. Pour egg mixture over the bread and berries, filling evenly to the rim.

Place the soufflé cups in a large ovenproof baking dish and pour boiling water into the dish until it reaches about halfway up the sides of the soufflé cups. Bake for 30 to 35 minutes, or until a cake tester or tooth-pick placed in the center of the puddings comes out clean. Remove from oven and allow to cool. These can be made one day ahead of the shower; simply refrigerate overnight and serve at room temperature. Just before serving, dust each top with powdered sugar.

Serves 8.

DOUBLE CHOCOLATE RASPBERRY CAKE

Tart, juicy raspberries are stacked between layers of rich chocolate cake for a delectable and colorful presentation. You can bake this cake the night before the shower and keep refrigerated overnight. Frost and decorate the cake the morning of the shower.

1 BOX CHOCOLATE CAKE MIX

3 EGGS

1/2 CUP VEGETABLE OIL

1/3 CUP WATER

6 OUNCES SEMISWEET
    CHOCOLATE CHIPS

1 RECIPE CHOCOLATE FROSTING
    (RECIPE FOLLOWS)

1/4 CUP RASPBERRY JAM

2 PINTS FRESH RASPBERRIES

Preheat oven to 350° F. Spray two 8-inch round cake pans with cooking spray. In a large bowl, combine the cake mix, eggs, oil, and water and beat with an electric mixer for about 2 minutes, until smooth and creamy.

Using a rubber spatula or spoon, fold the chocolate chips into the cake batter. Divide batter evenly between the two cake pans and bake for 30 minutes, or until a toothpick or cake tester placed in the center of the cakes comes out clean. Remove from oven and allow to cool in their pans. When cool, turn one cake out, round side down, on a flat serving platter or cake pedestal covered with two pieces of waxed paper, slightly overlapping in the center. If you prefer the cake to be perfectly flat on top, slice the rounded side off both layers before stacking.

Apply a thin layer of chocolate frosting to the top of the first layer, followed by a layer of raspberry jam. Dot approximately 1/4 cup of fresh raspberries on top of the jam, leaving spaces between berries. Carefully place the second layer of chocolate cake, rounded side up, or if top has been removed, bottom side up, gently aligning the two layers together. With an offset spatula or knife, spread a thin layer of frosting around the sides of the cake and add extra frosting until the sides are covered and smooth. Frost the top of the cake until covered and smooth. Finish the top and sides of the cake with the remaining raspberries.

Serves 10 to 12.

CHOCOLATE FROSTING

You can enhance the flavor of this frosting recipe with extracts of orange or mint if frosting a plain chocolate cake. Make this frosting up to two days in advance. Cover tightly and refrigerate until ready to use.

1/2 CUP UNSALTED BUTTER AT ROOM
    TEMPERATURE

3 CUPS POWDERED SUGAR

3 TABLESPOONS COCOA POWDER

4 TABLESPOONS HEAVY CREAM

1 TEASPOON VANILLA

In a work bowl with an electric mixer, cream the butter. Sift the sugar and cocoa powder together and gradually add it to the butter, beating well after each addition. Add the cream and vanilla and beat until well blended and fluffy.

POUND CAKE SQUARES WITH MIXED BERRIES

Little squares of cake make perfect individual portions. We used our favorite combination of berries picked at their peak, but feel free to use any fruit in season. Bake two days in advance and assemble a few hours before the party.

---

2 BOXES POUND CAKE MIX

6 TABLESPOONS BUTTER, MELTED

3 CUPS WHIPPING CREAM

1 CUP SUGAR

2 CUPS MIXED BERRIES (WE USED
    STRAWBERRIES, RASPBERRIES,
    AND BLUEBERRIES)

Bake each pound cake in a loaf pan according to package directions. Allow to cool. Using a large serrated knife, trim crusts off all sides of cake to make an even rectangle. Slice the rectangle in half lengthwise, then cut each piece in half lengthwise. Cut each long section crosswise three times to make 16 small squares. Repeat with second loaf.

Using a small serrated knife, cut a square from the center of each cube, leaving a 1/2-inch wall around the edges. Remove the cut sections carefully, making sure to leave enough cake in the bottom to hold the filling.

Place the squares on an unlined baking sheet. Brush the upper edges of the cake squares with the melted butter using a pastry brush. Place under broiler for a few minutes until lightly toasted, making sure to watch closely—the squares brown quickly. Remove from oven and let cool.

These can be made up to 2 days ahead. If storing, pound cake squares can be transferred to airtight containers or placed closely together on a baking sheet and covered with plastic wrap, and stored in the refrigerator.

Place the whipping cream in the bowl of an electric mixer and whip until soft peaks form. Add the sugar slowly and whip until slightly stiff. Place a spoonful of whipped cream into each square, topping with sliced and whole berries, and serve.

Makes 32 squares.

CHOCOLATE MOUSSE WITH RASPBERRIES

This dessert looks especially elegant presented in tall goblets or dessert flutes. Fresh, tart raspberries complement the sweetness of the chocolate. The mousse can be made the day before the shower. Assemble the goblets a few hours before the shower and keep chilled in the refrigerator.

---

32 OUNCES FRESH WHIPPING CREAM

1 CUP SUGAR

TWO 4-OUNCE PACKAGES INSTANT
  CHOCOLATE PUDDING MIX

2 PINTS FRESH RASPBERRIES, RINSED

20 SMALL DESSERT GOBLETS

In a large work bowl, whip the cream with an electric mixer. As cream begins to thicken, slowly add the sugar and continue to whip until soft peaks form. Add the pudding mix and whip just until well blended.

Place a few raspberries in the bottom of each glass. Spoon a layer of mousse over berries and repeat layering raspberries and mousse until the goblets are filled. Top with a few raspberries, cover with plastic wrap, and chill in refrigerator at least 1/2 hour or until serving.

Serves 20.

PRETTY PETAL PUNCH

Floating petals on top of this pretty punch adds color to the buffet table. Make sure you choose flowers that haven't been sprayed with chemicals.

ONE 64-OUNCE CARTON GUAVA JUICE

ONE 2-LITER BOTTLE GINGER ALE

ICE CUBE OR SHAPED MOLD, LIKE A
    HEART OR RING

PINK ROSE PETALS

Pour the guava juice and ginger ale into a large punch bowl. Add enough cubes to cover surface, and float rose petals on top.

Serves 20.

1 2 ③ 4 5

TROPICAL COCKTAILS

DECORATIONS AND FAVORS

    GARNISHES

    BAMBOO SAKE CUPS

    ORCHID BOUTONNIERES

    CRACKED COCONUT CUPS

COCKTAILS

    COLD SAKE SHOOTERS

    MANGO MARTINI

    RUM SPRITZER

HORS D'OEUVRES

    TROPICAL FRUIT SALAD IN CRACKED COCONUT CUPS

    SCALLOP SKEWERS

    SWEET AND SPICY SHRIMP SKEWERS

    SESAME CHICKEN CHUNKS WITH DIPPING SAUCE

    PLANTAIN CHIPS WITH TROPICAL SALSA

    STICKY RICE BALLS

This informal yet elegant shower with a tropical theme is perfect for a couple planning a honeymoon of sun and sand. Festive drinks and foods make great conversation pieces, and the informal buffet encourages socializing among a large and diverse group of people. You can use your garden in summer, as we have done, or bring it indoors for a tropical escape during the colder months. Possible gift themes include luggage, sporting equipment, camping gear, and travel accessories.

Designed for thirty guests, this menu offers a variety of tastes—sweet, spicy, rich, and tangy—and the small serving sizes allow for very creative presentation. Fry up batches of Plantain Chips and serve them with Tropical Fruit Salsa. Sticky Rice Balls rolled around bits of crystallized ginger are impressive when stacked into pyramids atop a large banana leaf. The Sweet and Spicy Shrimp Skewers feature delicate shrimp and sweet wedges of pineapple threaded on fresh bamboo shoots. Sesame Chicken Chunks are rolled in a coating of sesame seeds and served with a store-bought dipping sauce. Juicy and sweet Tropical Fruit Salads served in Cracked Coconut Cups are as much a part of the decorations as they are the menu. Plan to allow at least two or three of each hors d'oeuvre per person if your party falls between regular mealtimes. If you choose to throw the party during a mealtime, you should have enough on hand for three to four per person.

We used a variety of rich woods, shades of green, and subtle shades of orange, melon, and pink to evoke the flavor of the tropics. Bamboo, that quintessential tropical icon, is a constant theme, appearing in the serving trays, hors d'oeuvre picks, and sake cups. The little Orchid Boutonnieres come together quickly and make a fragrant party favor. A mixture of palm fronds, ti, philodendron, and banana leaves adorn the center of the buffet table. An inexpensive arrangement of tropical fruits adds color and texture.

We chose to throw this party at dusk so we could incorporate some outdoor lighting in the decorations. A soft, romantic glow emanates from lanterns on the branches of a fig tree over the buffet. Tiny flicks of light dance from coconut and bamboo candles. Tiki torches cast a wash of light across the space. If you need to light your party, don't worry about every corner of the garden; concentrate on areas where you would like guests to gather.

Presentation is everything at an hors d'oeuvres party. You might find serving ideas in your own kitchen—for example, round bamboo steamers are just the right size for a pile of Plantain Chips or Sesame Chicken Chunks. Line trays from your collection with large tropical leaves. Cracked Coconut Cups can hold dipping sauce and salsa, and Bamboo Sake Cups can be filled with an assortment of hors d'oeuvre picks.

We've limited the cocktail menu to a few simple specialties. In keeping with the tropical theme, we suggest good-quality rums and juices, sophisticated Mango Martinis, Sake Shooters, and a nonalcoholic iced tea. It's best to hire a bartender or enlist the help of a friend (not a party guest) in tending the bar. You don't want to spend all your time mixing drinks and stocking supplies, nor do you want any of your guests to take on those tasks.

Everything can be purchased and prepared in advance. Rent glasses if your budget permits, or pull together a few different types of glasses from your collection. On the day of the party, organize the glassware into neat rows on one side and arrange bottles of rum and vodka with the mixers at the other end. Keep sake, soda, and mineral water in a large bucket filled with ice, and store a large trash container under the table for quick clean-ups. Prepare an array of colorful garnishes and arrange them on the bar for adorning cocktails.

PUTTING IT TOGETHER

THREE OR FOUR DAYS AHEAD
Purchase tropical fruit for centerpiece, salad, and salsa
Set aside bar equipment and supplies
Make Bamboo Sake Cups

TWO DAYS AHEAD
Soak skewers in water
Prepare Dipping Sauce for Sesame Chicken Chunks
Pick up flowers and tropical foliage from florist
Shop for last-minute ingredients

THE DAY BEFORE
Make pulp for Mango Martinis
If possible, set up the table for the buffet and bar area; otherwise, allow extra time the morning of the shower
Move bar equipment and supplies to bar area
Marinate scallops and thread onto skewers
Make Sticky Rice Balls and Tropical Fruit Salsa
Marinate chicken for Sesame Chicken Chunks

THE MORNING OF THE SHOWER
Arrange a tropical fruit centerpiece
Prepare garnishes for cocktails
Make and set out Orchid Boutonnieres
Cut fruit for Tropical Fruit Salad
Make Plantain Chips
Crack coconut shells

A FEW HOURS BEFORE
Grill Scallop Skewers and Sweet and Spicy Shrimp Skewers
Sauté and bake Sesame Chicken Chunks
Buy ice for cocktails

JUST BEFORE THE SHOWER
Arrange hors d'oeuvres on buffet table
Start music and light candles (if desired)

GARNISHES

Garnishing plates and drinks makes them extra special and festive. Here are a variety of suggestions for a beautiful presentation.

———————————————

fresh bamboo shoots make great skewers and picks

mini paper umbrellas and paper fruit picks are inexpensive, colorful
and festive skewers and garnishes

bamboo picks can be found at gourmet or import shops in different sizes

bamboo or long, wooden skewers are an elegant and practical way to hold
grilled hors d'oeuvres

melon balls and sliced wedges of tropical fruit can be placed in the glass,
on the rim of a glass, or threaded onto a pick or skewer

fresh sprigs of mint are a cool accompaniment to iced tea or fruit salad

small dendrobium orchids and other tropical flowers can decorate
drinks as well as hors d'oeuvres

wet the rim of a glass and dip in sugar or colored sugar

tiny tropical leaves can be arranged on a platter of hors d'oeuvres

spirals of lemon or lime rind: use a zester to create long, curling rinds

Cracked Coconut Cups (page 61) and Bamboo Sake Cups (page 58) can be
used to hold drinks, sauces, garnishes, and picks

BAMBOO SAKE CUPS

Because bamboo is easily grown in many climates, you might be lucky enough to find a patch nearby. Otherwise, check with your local nursery or florist for fresh bamboo sources. For these cups, we used stalks of 1 1/2-inch-diameter bamboo, but you can use stalks as narrow as 1 inch. Giant bamboo of 3 or more inches in diameter is beautiful cut into shallow cups.

For 30 Bamboo Sake Cups you will need:

6 STALKS FRESH BAMBOO (EACH NODE EQUALS 1 CUP)

MITER SAW WITH A FINE-TOOTHED BLADE, SMALL HANDSAW, OR DREMEL WITH CUTTING BLADE

SANDPAPER

Set a stalk on a sturdy surface and cut through the bamboo approximately 3/4 inch under the node with a miter saw, handsaw, or Dremel. Each node (the solid barrier marked by a ring around the bamboo) along its length will form the bottom of one sake cup. Finish the cup by sawing the stalk 1 inch above the same node. If you're using larger-diameter bamboo, adjust the height so that approximately 1 ounce of liquid will fill the cup.

Lightly sand the top rim to smooth out rough edges. Fresh bamboo cups will stay green for about 1 week, then fade to a golden brown.

COLD SAKE SHOOTERS

Purchase your favorite sake and chill it thoroughly. Keep it on ice throughout the party.

ICE COLD SAKE

To make these drinks, simply fill Bamboo Sake Cups with ice cold sake and serve.

ORCHID BOUTONNIERES

Order a stem or two of dendrobium orchids from your local florist. Most stems have 10 to 12 flowers per stem.
They come in a variety of colors and are easy to make into little favors for your guests.

For 30 Orchid Boutonnieres you
will need:

DENDROBIUM ORCHIDS (TWO OR
    THREE STEMS, DEPENDING ON THE
    NUMBER OF FLOWERS PER STEM)

LIGHT GREEN FLORAL STEM TAPE

SPRAY BOTTLE

PEARL HEAD OR QUILTING PINS

Remove each orchid bloom from the main stem, leaving the smaller stem attached. Wrap each stem from top to bottom with floral stem tape, pulling the tape taut around each stem.

After the boutonnieres are made, mist the blooms with a spray bottle. Push a pin through the top of each stem and arrange the boutonnieres on a tray for guests to take as they enter the party.

CRACKED COCONUT CUPS

We used these cups to hold servings of Tropical Fruit Salad (page 64), but they are also perfect for presenting Mango Martinis (page 63), dipping sauce, salsa, condiments, and hors d'oeuvre picks. We recommend cracking the coconuts the morning of the shower and keeping them covered with a damp paper towel so they won't dry out.

For 30 Cracked Coconut Cups you will need:

15 COCONUTS (EACH COCONUT WILL MAKE 2 CUPS)

AWL OR ICE PICK

HAMMER

SCREWDRIVER

PAPER TOWELS

Working outside on a hard surface, place a coconut on an old towel and use the ice pick to pierce the "eye" (dark dot) at one end. This will release pressure from the inside of the coconut, making it easier to crack open. Allow the liquid to drain out and reserve for another use, or discard.

Lay the coconut on its side and hit it hard with the hammer. Find a crack in the shell and wedge the screwdriver inside. Hit the end of the screwdriver with the hammer continuously until the coconut is completely broken in half. The jagged edges give the cups a rustic quality. Cover the flesh of the coconut with moistened paper towels until ready to use. Repeat with the remaining coconuts.

MANGO MARTINI

This fresh and fruity version of the sophisticated martini has a wonderful consistency. The mango pulp can be made the day before and refrigerated in an airtight container. Store it in a large pitcher at the bar until it's ready to be mixed.

---

3 FRESH MANGOS, CUT INTO CHUNKS

1 CUP SUGAR

1 CUP WATER

CITRON VODKA

ORANGE LIQUEUR (SUCH AS
    COINTREAU OR TRIPLE SEC)

1 CUP CRUSHED ICE

To make the mango pulp, place the fresh mango chunks into a food processor and process until very smooth. This is enough pulp for approximately 12 Mango Martinis.

To make the simple syrup, place the sugar and water in a small saucepan and cook over medium heat, stirring until sugar dissolves and liquid is clear. Do not boil. Allow to cool and store in refrigerator until ready to use.

To mix a Mango Martini, place 1 ounce each mango pulp, simple syrup, and vodka, plus 1/2 ounce orange liqueur in a blender. Add 1 cup crushed ice and blend until smooth. Serve in a classic martini stem glass or Cracked Coconut Cup and garnish with a colorful paper umbrella or tiny skewer of fruit.

RUM SPRITZER

With so many tropical juices available in supermarkets, why not put them to use and make instant exotic cocktails? Choose a few bottles of your favorite juice and use it to mix with dark or golden imported rum.

ICE CUBES

DARK OR GOLDEN RUM

TROPICAL FRUIT JUICE

LIME WEDGES

Fill a cocktail glass with ice cubes. Pour the rum over ice and fill glass with fruit juice. Garnish with a lime wedge.

TROPICAL FRUIT SALAD IN CRACKED COCONUT CUPS

The Cracked Coconut Cups (page 61) make a charming serving bowl for this colorful salad. The fruits we have chosen are classic tropical fruits, but feel free to substitute with other available fresh fruits.

---

3 PAPAYAS, PEELED, SEEDED,
    AND SLICED

3 CUPS PINEAPPLE, CUT INTO CHUNKS

6 KIWI, PEELED AND SLICED

3 CUPS WATERMELON, SHAPED
    INTO BALLS

3 PINTS STRAWBERRIES

30 SPRIGS MINT

Arrange the fresh fruit in the coconut halves. Garnish with the mint.

If desired, a quick dressing can be made by combining 1/2 cup honey and 1/2 cup lime juice. Pour the dressing over the fruit and lightly toss to coat evenly before arranging in bowls.

Serves 30.

SCALLOP SKEWERS

Prepare the skewers the day before the shower and store in the refrigerator. They can be grilled a few hours before guests arrive, but keep them warm until serving.

For the sauce:

$1/2$ CUP RICE WINE VINEGAR

$1/4$ CUP SOY SAUCE

$1/4$ CUP LIGHT MISO

4 GARLIC CLOVES, PEELED AND MINCED

$1/8$ CUP FRESH GINGER, PEELED AND MINCED

For the skewers:

15 GREEN ONIONS

30 LARGE SCALLOPS

To make the sauce, combine all the sauce ingredients. Save half for dipping and use half for brushing on skewers while grilling.

If using wooden skewers, soak them in water for 30 minutes before grilling. Cut the green onions into 2-inch lengths, using only the white and light green sections. Place 1 scallop and 1 piece of green onion on each skewer. Grill on an outdoor grill or grill pan over medium heat until scallops are just opaque, about 2 minutes for each side, brushing with sauce.

Makes 30 skewers.

SWEET AND SPICY SHRIMP SKEWERS

This hearty appetizer combines a spicy red curry paste with the mellow flavor of coconut milk to make a quick marinade for the shrimp. Present them threaded on thin bamboo shoots with chunks of sweet pineapple. If you don't want to work the grill during the party, these skewers can be grilled a few hours beforehand and served at room temperature.

2 TABLESPOONS RED CURRY PASTE

1/2 CUP CANNED COCONUT MILK

3 DOZEN LARGE SHRIMP, PEELED AND
   DEVEINED

1 LARGE FRESH PINEAPPLE, TRIMMED,
   CORED, AND CUT INTO 1-INCH
   CHUNKS

In a small bowl, whisk together curry paste and coconut milk. Thread one shrimp and one pineapple chunk onto each skewer. Brush each skewer with coconut sauce and grill over medium heat, about 4 to 5 minutes per side, or until shrimp is opaque. Turn frequently and continue to brush with sauce.

Makes 36 skewers.

SESAME CHICKEN CHUNKS WITH DIPPING SAUCE

Marinating the chicken breasts the night before infuses the meat with flavor. To save time, select your favorite
Asian dipping sauce at a grocery store and dilute with mirin (a sweet rice cooking wine found in the Asian food section)
until it has a smooth consistency. We used a store-bought plum sauce for this recipe.

1/4 CUP ORANGE JUICE CONCENTRATE

1/4 CUP SEASONED RICE VINEGAR

2 TABLESPOONS SESAME OIL

2 TABLESPOONS LIME JUICE

1 TEASPOON CRUSHED RED PEPPER

8 BONELESS CHICKEN BREASTS,
SLICED LENGTHWISE IN HALF, OR
15 CHICKEN TENDERLOINS

1/2 CUP SESAME SEEDS

BOTTLED PLUM SAUCE FOR DIPPING

Combine the first five ingredients in a large bowl. Add the chicken breasts and marinate for at least 1 hour, or preferably overnight. Preheat oven to 400° F, and prepare a baking sheet with nonstick spray.

Spread the sesame seeds on a plate or shallow platter. Remove the chicken slices from the marinade, shake off excess, and roll in sesame seeds until well coated. Sauté the coated strips in a large nonstick skillet until light, golden, and cooked almost through.

Transfer the cooked chicken to a baking sheet and bake for 20 minutes. Remove and let cool. Refrigerate if not serving immediately. Slice the chicken strips into large bite-size chunks and serve with bamboo hors d'oeuvre picks and your favorite dipping sauce.

Serves 30.

PLANTAIN CHIPS WITH TROPICAL SALSA

Plantains, native to tropical regions, are commonly found in the produce section of the supermarket. The hard green ones are best for chips. They can be difficult to peel, but using a knife to cut back the skin will make this task easier. The salsa, made with the freshest ingredients, should be prepared a day ahead to give the flavors a chance to blend.

For the chips:

6 FIRM GREEN PLANTAINS

PEANUT OIL FOR FRYING

KOSHER SALT

For the salsa:

1 CUP MANGO, $1/2$-INCH DICE

1 CUP TOMATO, SEEDED AND CHOPPED
INTO $1/2$-INCH DICE

$1/2$ CUP RED ONION, $1/2$-INCH DICE

$1/2$ CUP JICAMA OR CUCUMBER,
$1/2$-INCH DICE

$1/2$ CUP KIWI OR AVOCADO, $1/2$-INCH
DICE

2 JALAPEÑO PEPPERS, SEEDED AND
MINCED

$1/4$ CUP CILANTRO, CHOPPED

JUICE OF 2 ORANGES

JUICE OF 3 LIMES

SALT AND PEPPER TO TASTE

To make the chips, peel the plantains and slice diagonally into $1/4$-inch-thick pieces. Pour 1 inch of peanut oil in a skillet on medium heat. Test the oil with a slice of plantain to make sure it is hot enough to fry without smoking; adjust heat if necessary. Have several layers of paper towel laid out nearby.

Place approximately 8 plantain slices in skillet to fry for about 1 minute, remove, and lay out on paper towels. Using the flat side of a meat tenderizer, pound each plantain slice to soften. Fry the pounded slices again for about 2 minutes, until they start to brown at the edges. Drain on fresh paper towels. Sprinkle with kosher salt to taste. Repeat until all slices are fried.

Makes about 120 chips.

To make the salsa, toss all the fruit, vegetables, and juices in a bowl and season with salt and pepper.

STICKY RICE BALLS

Be sure to make plenty of these so you can stack them into small pyramid shapes around the buffet table. Each rice ball has a small surprise in the center. We used crystallized ginger, but green onion, dried fruit, or diced ham is equally delicious. The rice balls can be made a day ahead and kept in an airtight container in the refrigerator.

---

2 TABLESPOONS VEGETABLE OIL

1 CUP SHORT-GRAIN RICE

2 CUPS VEGETABLE STOCK, HEATED

1/2 CUP SESAME SEEDS, TOASTED

1/2 CUP BLACK SESAME SEEDS

8 OUNCES CRYSTALLIZED GINGER,
    CUT INTO 1/2-INCH CHUNKS

In a large nonstick skillet, heat the oil over medium-high heat. Sauté the rice, making sure all the grains are lightly coated with oil. Lower heat to medium and add the vegetable stock about a half cup at a time, stirring to let it absorb before adding more. Continue cooking and stirring for about 20 minutes, until rice is tender. Remove rice from heat and allow to cool. Pour the toasted and black sesame seeds on separate plates and set aside.

Roll a spoonful of rice around a piece of ginger and form it into a ball about 1 inch in diameter. Roll the rice ball in the sesame seeds until it is completely coated, alternating colors for each ball. Repeat with the remaining ingredients. If you're making these a day ahead, place them in an airtight container and store in the refrigerator until ready to serve.

To serve, make a rice ball pyramid by placing the balls in a square formation on a leaf-covered serving platter. Each side of the square should have four balls. Fill in the square. Stack another layer on top of the square just in from the outside edge. Each side of this square should have one fewer rice ball on each side. Continue until a pyramid shape is formed.

Makes 30 pieces.

1 2 3 ④ 5

A DAY OF BEAUTY

DECORATIONS AND FAVORS

SAGE ASTRINGENT

HERBAL STEAM POUCHES

BATH SALTS

TERRY CLOTH BEAUTY BAGS

CORRUGATED SOUP CUPS

MENU

EASY MISO SOUP

SPA NOODLE SALAD

SHRIMP SPRING ROLLS WITH PEANUT DIPPING SAUCE

FORTUNE COOKIES

GREEN TEA

MINERAL WATER WITH LEMON SLICES

For the bride, the wedding day carries many expectations. With stress and anxiety at its peak, she's probably ready for some pampering with a select group of friends. Why not treat her to "A Day of Beauty"?

Beauty rituals have long been integral to the wedding traditions of many cultures. This luxurious shower offers guests an opportunity to indulge in some good food and an afternoon of pampering. If your budget allows, hire a professional to come to the site and give guests manicures, pedicures, or facials. If not, gather together the equipment for these treatments, and let guests pamper themselves. Either way, this intimate party is a lovely way for guests to relax and take time for themselves.

We designed the easy-to-prepare menu for eight to be completely portable, giving the host the option of throwing this shower at home, at the bride's home, or in a hotel room (perfect for a day-before-the-wedding shower). Light, fresh ingredients are prepared with an Asian influence, and the menu is healthy and flavorful. Crisp carrots and cabbage combine with spicy and nutty soba noodles in a Spa Noodle Salad. Thick chunks of miso-soaked tofu and green onion slivers float in steaming Easy Miso Soup that can be made in advance and reheated just before serving in Corrugated Soup Cups. Translucent sheets of rice paper are filled with delicate shrimp, crunchy carrots, and bean thread noodles, then rolled into Shrimp Spring Rolls and served with a Peanut Dipping Sauce. A pot of aromatic green tea can be served in tall ceramic cups along with a decanter of mineral water lightly flavored with lemon slices. And for dessert, a box of crunchy fortune cookies.

Minimal last-minute preparation is the key to being able to enjoy relaxing with your guests. We thought it would be both fun and practical to package food in portable boxes and containers—perfect if the site is the bride's home or hotel room, and handy no matter what the location. Sturdy white take-out containers fitted with metal handles hold both the Spring Rolls and Spa Noodle Salad. Fortune cookies are piled inside a square wooden box. The Easy Miso Soup will stay hot in a thermos, ready to serve in the decorative Corrugated Soup Cups. The boxed lunches, or *bentos,* can be set out for guests to enjoy at their leisure.

Creating the serenity and calmness of an oasis retreat takes minimal effort. Think clean and simple paired with pure luxury. If you're hosting this shower at home, set aside time to clear away excess clutter. Improvise with things you have around the house—use wooden and metal trays to hold steaming cups of green tea, groupings of candles, or gardenias in bowls of water. Arrange stacks of plush towels with the tools needed for manicures and beauty treatments. Lighting should be soft and natural, so turn off any harsh fluorescents. Light candles or just use natural light, but make lamplight available near the manicure station.

The homemade beauty treatments are in keeping with the theme of the home spa. As a special gift to close friends or bridesmaids, fill handmade Terry Cloth Beauty Bags with an extra supply of the homemade spa treatments, plus a bottle of nail polish and lipstick to wear during the wedding. Package Bath Salts in metal tins tied with tiny wooden scoops. Fill small apothecary bottles with Sage Astringent, and finish with a metal rim tag listing ingredients and instructions. The beauty treatments, especially the astringent, should be made a couple weeks before the shower. It will take just a few hours to prepare the treatments, and an additional hour or two to package the favors in the beauty bags.

FOUR TO SIX WEEKS OR MORE AHEAD

Book professional beauty services (manicure, pedicure, masseuse, hairdresser, etc.)

TWO WEEKS AHEAD

Start making Sage Astringent

Make Herbal Steam Pouches

Purchase or sew Terry Cloth Beauty Bags

Order gardenias and stephanotis from florist

ONE WEEK AHEAD

Make Bath Salts

Package beauty treatments and put into Terry Cloth Beauty Bags

Confirm bookings with beauty professionals

Make Corrugated Soup Cups

TWO DAYS AHEAD

Launder and stack towels and robes

Shop for last-minute ingredients

THE DAY BEFORE

Make Peanut Dipping Sauce

Arrange furniture and set out supplies for beauty treatments

THE MORNING OF THE SHOWER

Chop vegetables for Shrimp Spring Rolls and Spa Noodle Salad

Float gardenias in water

A FEW HOURS BEFORE

Make Easy Miso Soup and Spa Noodle Salad

Roll ingredients into Shrimp Spring Rolls

JUST BEFORE THE SHOWER

Pour water into pitcher or decanter with lemon and ice

Set containers of food on table

Boil water and brew tea

Light candles

Start music

SAGE ASTRINGENT

You'll need to start this tonic at least two weeks ahead of the party, but it's well worth the effort. Splashed on the skin, it is refreshing and reviving. Packaged in small apothecary bottles (available at medical, beauty, or aromatherapy supply stores), it makes a beautiful shower favor. The tincture of benzoin will help preserve the astringent and keep the sage leaf fresh.

For two 2-ounce bottles of Sage Astringent you will need:

1/2 CUP FRESH SAGE

16-OUNCE BOTTLE OR JAR

1/2 CUP VODKA

2 PAPER COFFEE FILTERS

5–6 DROPS TINCTURE OF BENZOIN
   (A PRESERVATIVE)

FUNNEL

TWO 2-OUNCE APOTHECARY BOTTLES

2 FRESH SAGE LEAVES

SMALL ROUND TAG OR LABEL

Place 1/4 cup of the fresh sage in the large bottle and pour the vodka over it. Cap the bottle and let stand for 1 week.

Strain the mixture through a coffee filter into a bowl. Place the remaining 1/4 cup sage in the same bottle, return the strained liquid to the bottle, and let stand another week.

Strain the mixture through a coffee filter again and add the tincture of benzoin to the strained liquid. Using the funnel, divide the liquid between the apothecary bottles. Place a single sage leaf in each bottle. Cap the bottles and label.

Makes two 2-ounce bottles.

HERBAL STEAM POUCHES

These little pouches are filled with a mixture of herbs. When dropped into a bowl of hot water, the steam from the herbs releases a delicate fragrance and works to purify the complexion.

For 16 Herbal Steam Pouches you will need:

4 OUNCES LAVENDER

4 OUNCES CALENDULA

2 OUNCES CINNAMON BARK

4 OUNCES CHAMOMILE

SIXTEEN 5-INCH SQUARES OF CHEESE-
  CLOTH OR LOOSE-WEAVE COTTON

COTTON KITCHEN STRING

Combine the lavender, calendula, cinnamon bark, and chamomile in a small bowl, mixing gently with hands. Place 2 tablespoons of the herb mixture in the center of one cheesecloth square, and bundle so mixture forms a ball shape. Cut a small piece of the string and tie a double knot or small bow around the ball of herbs, leaving the corners of the cheese-cloth loose at the top.

BATH SALTS

Mixing just a few different kinds of salts together results in a soothing treat for the bath. There are many ways to mix bath salts, and the end result will vary according to the ingredients used. We offer three different mixtures to try. Packaged in metal tins, the salts make fragrant favors.

For the Bath Salts you will need a combination of the following ingredients:

EPSOM SALT

BAKING SODA

TABLE SALT

SEA SALT

ESSENTIAL OIL (SUCH AS GARDENIA, LAVENDER, OR ROSE)

Combine 2 cups Epsom salt, $1\frac{1}{3}$ cups baking soda, $\frac{2}{3}$ cup table salt, and a few drops of essential oil.

Combine $2\frac{2}{3}$ cups sea salt, $1\frac{1}{3}$ cup Epsom salt, and a few drops of essential oil.

Combine 2 cups sea salt, 2 cups baking soda, and a few drops of essential oil.

Each mixture makes 4 cups.

To package the bath salts in tins, divide a salt mixture equally into eight 4-ounce tins and cover with the lids. Label each tin with the name and formula of the salt mixture using premade labels, or make your own labels by cutting sticky-back paper slightly smaller in diameter than the lid of the tin.

TERRY CLOTH BEAUTY BAGS

These favor bags can be made in just a few hours on a sewing machine. If you're short on time, look for inexpensive cosmetic bags at a beauty supply or discount store. Finished bags are 8 inches by 10 inches, large enough to hold a variety of beauty items, such as Bath Salts (page 84), Herbal Steam Pouches (page 83), and Sage Astringent (page 80).

For each Terry Cloth Beauty Bag you will need:

TERRY CLOTH FABRIC, 22 BY 10
    INCHES

SEWING MACHINE

IRON

STITCH RIPPER

1 YARD COTTON TWILL TAPE

SAFETY PIN (OPTIONAL)

Fold the fabric crosswise, right sides together. Stitch the two long sides closed 1/4 inch in from the edge. Press the seams flat with a warm iron.

Turn down the top edge 1/4 inch around the mouth of the bag and press. Turn this edge down 1 inch and press. Stitch around the bottom edge. Turn the bag right side out.

Using a stitch ripper or manicure scissors, carefully snip the stitches of one side seam from the top edge of the bag to just above the seam that runs around the bag—about 1 inch. Gently open up the small gap.

Thread the twill tape through the small gap on the side of the bag. A safety pin fastened through the leading edge of the tape will make the threading easier.

CORRUGATED SOUP CUPS

White paper drink or soup cups can be found at party, restaurant supply, or discount stores. Wrapped with a strip of corrugated paper and tied with cord, they take on a modern Asian flair. The extra layer of corrugated paper keeps the soup hot but not the cups, making them easier to handle.

For 8 Corrugated Soup Cups you will need:

WHITE CORRUGATED PAPER

8 WHITE PAPER DRINK OR SOUP CUPS

SCISSORS

SCOTCH TAPE

TAN FABRIC BEADING CORD

Wrap the corrugated paper around a cup, leaving a 1/2-inch overlap, and trim the paper to size. Secure one end of the paper along the length of the cup with scotch tape. Wrap the corrugated paper around the cup, securing with a length of cord knotted around the cup. Repeat for additional cups.

EASY MISO SOUP

Miso is a high-protein, low-fat paste made from soybeans. This flavorful soup can be made the day of the party and ladled into Corrugated Soup Cups (page 87). Reheat in the microwave just before serving.

10 CUPS WATER

1/4 CUP SWEET WHITE MISO

3 TABLESPOONS DARK MISO

8 OUNCES EXTRA-FIRM TOFU, CUT INTO 1/2-INCH DICE

1/2 CUP SLICED GREEN ONION

Bring 1 cup of the water to a boil in a small saucepan. Pour over both miso pastes and dissolve with small wire whisk or fork until blended. Bring the remaining 9 cups water to a boil in large saucepan and whisk in the dissolved miso until blended. Reduce heat to medium, add the tofu, and stir to combine. Can be served or ladled into cups for reheating in microwave. Top with the sliced green onion.

Serves 8.

SPA NOODLE SALAD

This delicious salad is made with Japanese soba noodles, which are found in the Asian section of most large supermarkets. If you can't find soba noodles, you can substitute linguine. We suggest serving portions in white paper take-out containers so guests can easily help themselves. The salad can be made a day in advance and refrigerated until ready to serve.

For the dressing:

4 TABLESPOONS GINGER, MINCED

2 TABLESPOONS MIRIN

3 TABLESPOONS SOY SAUCE

$1/2$ CUP SEASONED RICE VINEGAR

3 TABLESPOONS SESAME OIL

For the salad:

THREE 10-OUNCE PACKAGES SOBA
     NOODLES

4 CARROTS, PEELED AND CUT INTO
     MATCHSTICKS

8 GREEN ONIONS, CUT INTO MATCH
     STICKS

2 RED OR YELLOW PEPPERS, CORED
     AND CUT INTO MATCHSTICKS

1 CUP CILANTRO, CHOPPED

1 CABBAGE, GREEN OR PURPLE,
     THINLY SLICED

4 OUNCES PEANUTS, CHOPPED

To make the dressing, combine all the dressing ingredients in a small bowl and set aside.

Bring a large pot of water to a boil for the noodles. Cook noodles for 5 minutes, until al dente. Drain in colander and rinse under cold water until cool. Place noodles in a large bowl and add the carrots, green onion, peppers, and cilantro. Toss with the dressing, making sure all noodles are well coated. At this point, the salad can be refrigerated for up to one day.

To assemble, place cabbage on the bottom of each take-out container, followed by seasoned noodles, and top with peanuts.

Serves 8.

SHRIMP SPRING ROLLS WITH PEANUT DIPPING SAUCE

Translucent sheets of rice paper hint at the fresh ingredients inside these little pouches. Because the paper is very fragile, make sure to buy extra to work with. Spring rolls can be made up to three hours before serving.

For the Peanut Dipping Sauce:

2 TABLESPOONS MINCED FRESH GINGER

1/4 CUP HOT WATER

1/2 CUP PEANUT BUTTER

2 TABLESPOONS SOY SAUCE

4 TABLESPOONS RICE VINEGAR

2 TABLESPOONS SWEET WHITE MISO

1/4 TEASPOON RED PEPPER FLAKES

For the Spring Rolls:

3 OUNCES BEAN THREAD NOODLES,
    COOKED AND DRAINED

1 CUP FINELY SHREDDED CABBAGE

1/3 CUP GRATED CARROT

1/4 CUP SLICED GREEN ONION

1/4 CUP SESAME SEEDS, TOASTED

16 CILANTRO LEAVES, WHOLE

16 MINT LEAVES, WHOLE

1 POUND SHRIMP, COOKED, PEELED,
    AND SPLIT IN HALF LENGTHWISE

SIXTEEN 6-INCH ROUND SHEETS RICE
    PAPER

To make the dipping sauce, combine first six ingredients in a small bowl and season to taste with red pepper flakes. Set aside.

In a large bowl combine the bean thread noodles, cabbage, carrot, green onion, and sesame seeds. Place the cilantro, mint, and shrimp in separate work bowls nearby.

To soften the rice paper, fill a pie plate or shallow baking dish with tepid water. Place two or three rice paper sheets in the water and allow to soak about 45 seconds to 1 minute. Remove one at a time and carefully stack between sheets of paper towel. Continue soaking and draining until you have 16 softened rice sheets.

Turn over the stack and begin working from the bottom of the stack first. Place a softened rice paper sheet on a clean work surface. On the bottom third of the sheet, pile 1/4 cup of the noodle mixture. Just above noodles, place a shrimp half, skin side down, and top with a cilantro leaf and mint leaf. Fold bottom of paper up over noodle mixture, then fold each side toward the center, rolling gently and as tightly as possible from the bottom until completely rolled. Place rolls seam side down on a plate and continue until all ingredients have been used.

Keep assembled rolls under wet paper towels covered with plastic wrap. Store at room temperature up to 3 hours; do not refrigerate.

Serves 8.

1 2 3 4 ⑤

BEACH BARBECUE

DECORATIONS AND FAVORS

STARFISH INVITATIONS

COLORFUL CANOPIES

PICNIC TABLECLOTHS

FAVOR BUCKETS

MENU

GRILLED AHI TUNA BURGERS WITH WASABI MAYONNAISE

LEMON CHICKEN BREASTS

BLACK BEAN AND ROASTED CORN SALAD

RED AND YELLOW TOMATO SALAD CAPRESE

RUSTIC PEACH TART

ASSORTMENT OF BOTTLED DRINKS

The barbecue is perhaps the most nontraditional shower in this book. It's a terrific choice for a couple interested in an informal party with good friends and fun activities (other than gift opening). We chose a beach—good for sandcastle building and water sports—but many other locations will work equally well: a park, lakeshore, or backyard (especially one with a pool). The Starfish Invitations hint at the playfulness of the shower and notify guests that the order of the day is fun in the sun.

Hosting a shower in a public place takes a lot of planning ahead, but it is an excellent choice for a large party and for a host whose home can't accommodate a crowd. Be sure to research the location thoroughly before deciding. Find out if there are any restrictions on the use of grills, alcoholic beverages, and certain types of recreational activities such as surfing or fishing. Check on the availability of parking and on facilities for fresh water and restrooms. Be aware of the limitations, and adjust accordingly.

The menu, designed for thirty people, is completely portable, requires minimal preparation on site, and can be altered according to your needs. The flavors are bold and zesty, and built around the tastes of the season. The Red and Yellow Tomato Salad Caprese, enhanced with basil and dressed in a mustard vinaigrette, makes the most of summer tomatoes. Fresh cilantro accents the vibrant Black Bean and Roasted Corn Salad. The Grilled Ahi Tuna Burger reinterprets the classic American burger with a hearty and flavorful tuna steak topped with a tangy Wasabi Mayonnaise. Lemon Chicken Breasts marinated for a few days in a garlicky vinaigrette are infused with flavor. You can prebake the breasts at home and finish them off on the grill. For dessert, the Rustic Peach Tart features the pick of the crop baked inside a flaky crust.

To match the warm weather, outdoor location, and flavorful food, we decorated in bright orange and hot pink. We purchased yards of inexpensive cotton fabric in both colors and made Colorful Canopies and Picnic Tablecloths, even napkins and sarongs for the guests. Hot pink utensil sets wrapped with orange checked napkins are tied with jute twine and stuffed inside an orange bucket at the beginning of the buffet. Inexpensive rattan plate holders can be lined with a square of parchment paper and used as plates, making cleanup easy. A large galvanized tub filled with ice holds an assortment of bottled drinks and water, and invites guests to help themselves.

An open outdoor location calls for a shady area to protect both food and guests from the hot sun. Fashioned simply from squares of fabric and bamboo poles, the canopies are a festive and functional way to provide shade and to designate the eating area. When guests arrive, the bright canopies show them exactly where to go.

Since a shower of this nature will likely be an all-day event, it's a nice idea to provide guests with some goodies they might not have thought to bring. The bright orange Favor Buckets are filled with treats—an extra bottle of water, sunscreen, crackers, and candies. You might also consider supplying stacks of rolled beach towels for guests who might forget theirs. Encourage guests to bring along their favorite outdoor recreational equipment— Frisbees, paddle balls, boogie boards and surfboards, fishing poles, rafts, and floating tubes.

For the guests of honor, consider a gift theme centered around the home and garden. Buckets, storage bins, or pails filled with new tools are ideal for a couple buying a home together. A split wood bushel basket chock-full of gardening tools is a great gift for a couple who spends time puttering in the backyard.

Don't Forget to Pack: Cooler for perishables. Charcoal, lighter fluid, and matches. Grilling tools, knife, and small cutting board. Olive oil for the grill. Bottle opener. Trash bags and paper towels. Jugs of bottled water. Garden trowel and safety pins for canopies.

FOUR WEEKS AHEAD
Make Starfish Invitations and mail
Make Colorful Canopies and Picnic Tablecloths

FOUR DAYS AHEAD
Make Favor Buckets

TWO DAYS AHEAD
Marinate Lemon Chicken Breasts
Make Black Bean and Roasted Corn Salad
Make dressing for Tomato Salad Caprese
Prepare and store condiments for Ahi Tuna Burgers

ONE DAY AHEAD
Load car with equipment, decorations, and supplies for shower
Prebake Lemon Chicken and transfer to portable container
Chop tomatoes for Tomato Salad Caprese
Make marinade for Ahi Tuna Burgers
Bake Rustic Peach Tart

THE MORNING OF THE SHOWER
Purchase fresh tuna steaks from fish market
Load food into car
Set up party location (grill, tables, canopies, tablecloths)

A FEW HOURS BEFORE
Slice lemons for chicken
Purchase ice

JUST BEFORE THE SHOWER
Transfer food into serving dishes, dress Tomato Salad Caprese
Assemble condiment platter for burgers
Pour ice over bottled drinks in ice bucket
Start charcoal on grill

STARFISH INVITATIONS

Kraft boxes lined with excelsior cushion a delicate starfish for its journey through the mail system. You should
be able to find all of these supplies, including the starfish and excelsior (a finely shredded wood used for packing),
at your local arts-and-crafts store.

For each Starfish Invitation you will need:

EXCELSIOR IN NATURAL COLOR

5-BY-6-INCH KRAFT PAPER BOX
    WITH LID

MANILA MAILING TAG

PINK FELT TIP PEN

STARFISH, APPROXIMATELY 4 3/4-INCH
    ACROSS

KRAFT PAPER SHIPPING TAPE

Place excelsior in the box. Write party information on the tag using the felt tip pen. Place the starfish in box on top of excelsior. Attach the mailing tag to the starfish. Seal the lid onto the box with a strip of kraft paper shipping tape. Address and mail the boxes.

COLORFUL CANOPIES

These quick and easy canopies will protect your food (and your guests) from the hot sun. If you don't have a sewing machine, the canopies can be left unfinished at the edges. These directions are for three square canopies using fabric that is 54 inches wide, but you can make the canopies any size you like.

To make 3 Colorful Canopies you will need:

TAPE MEASURE

SCISSORS

3 YARDS LIGHTWEIGHT COTTON
FABRIC IN HOT PINK

1 1/2 YARDS LIGHTWEIGHT COTTON
FABRIC IN BRIGHT ORANGE

SEWING MACHINE (OPTIONAL)

GARDEN TROWEL OR SMALL SHOVEL

12 BAMBOO STAKES (1-INCH DIAME-
TER), CUT INTO 7-FOOT LENGTHS

Measure and cut the pink fabric into two 54-inch squares. Hem the edges of the pink squares and the orange square with a sewing machine, or just leave the edges unfinished.

At the picnic location, choose a site for your canopies and lay the fabric squares out on the sand or lawn. Fold each corner back a few inches and, using the garden trowel, mark the sand or lawn at the center of each fold. Remove the fabric squares and dig holes at your markings. Tie the corners of one canopy to four bamboo stakes and drive the stakes into the holes. Repeat with the remaining canopies and bamboo stakes.

Note: If you are digging in sod, score and remove circle-shaped sod plugs the same size in diameter as the holes you will be digging. Once the bamboo poles have been secured into place, make a cut in the radius of each sod plug and fit into place around each pole. This will fill in the space around the bamboo poles, leaving a neat and uniform appearance in the lawn. After the party, use the plugs to repair the holes you dug.

PICNIC TABLECLOTHS

These tablecloths are really just simple cloth squares. Smaller squares in opposite colors placed on top
of larger squares create a two-toned tablecloth. These instructions are designed for three 30-inch square tables, but
you can make the tablecloths any size you like.

To make 3 Picnic Tablecloths you will need:

TAPE MEASURE

SCISSORS

11 1/2 YARDS LIGHTWEIGHT BRIGHT
    ORANGE COTTON, 36 INCHES WIDE

8 YARDS LIGHTWEIGHT HOT PINK
    COTTON FABRIC, 46 INCHES WIDE

SEWING MACHINE

IRON

Measure and cut the orange fabric into four 92-by-46-inch pieces, and
one 46-inch square. Measure and cut the pink fabric into two 92-by-46-
inch pieces, plus two 46-inch squares.

Stitch a 1/4-inch hem around the edges of the three fabric squares and
set aside. These are your tablecloth toppers.

Match the right sides of two long pieces of orange fabric and stitch along
the long edge. Press the seam open. You will have a 92-inch square.
Repeat with the two remaining orange pieces, and then with the two pink
pieces. Stitch a 1/4-inch hem around the edges of these large squares.

Cover your tables with the three large squares and top with a smaller
square in the contrasting color.

These colorful buckets filled with essentials for the beach will ensure that your guests enjoy their day in the sun. They're easy to assemble and make great decorations. Make one for each person and line them up on a table for guests to take as they arrive.

For each Favor Bucket you will need:

METAL BUCKET, APPROXIMATELY
    6 INCHES TALL AND 6 INCHES
    IN DIAMETER

ORANGE SPRAY PAINT (ONE 14-OUNCE
    CAN WILL COVER SIX BUCKETS)

TWO CELLOPHANE BAGS

GOLDFISH CRACKERS

SISAL TWINE

ORANGE GUMMY RINGS

DOT STICKER

FABRIC HANKY (YOU CAN TEAR LEFT
    OVER MATERIAL FROM THE
    CANOPIES INTO A 16-INCH
    SQUARE)

TRIAL-SIZE BOTTLE OF SUNSCREEN

SMALL BOTTLE OF WATER

If necessary, remove the handle from the bucket. Spray paint the bucket orange, applying two coats for best results. Allow the bucket to dry overnight.

Fill one cellophane bag with goldfish crackers and tie closed with sisal twine. Fill the other bag with gummy rings and seal the bag closed with the dot sticker. Line the bucket with the fabric hanky. Arrange sunscreen, bottle of water, crackers, and gummy rings in the bucket.

GRILLED AHI TUNA BURGERS

This is the coastal version of the classic American burger. Make the marinade the day before and add to tuna steaks about fifteen minutes before grilling. Serve with an assortment of condiments: fresh tomato, Wasabi Mayonnaise (recipe follows), spicy mustards, paper-thin slices of red onion, crisp sprouts, and leaves of bibb lettuce.

1/2 CUP SOY SAUCE

1/2 CUP SEASONED RICE VINEGAR

4 TABLESPOONS FRESH GINGER, CHOPPED

2 TABLESPOONS GARLIC, CHOPPED

2 TABLESPOONS SESAME OIL

1 CUP VEGETABLE OIL

30 TUNA STEAKS (3 TO 4 OUNCES EACH)

30 ROLLS SUCH POPPY SEED, HAMBURGER BUNS, OR SLICED FRENCH BREAD

Combine the first six ingredients. Store in a jar or airtight container in refrigerator until you are ready to transport. Place the tuna steaks in heavy plastic resealable bags or containers.

Before grilling, pour the soy mixture over the steaks and let stand for 15 minutes. Bring grill to medium-high heat and sear steaks on each side (2 to 4 minutes, depending on desired doneness). While steaks are grilling, toast rolls or bread slices lightly around the outside edges of the barbecue and set aside on serving platter. Remove tuna steaks directly onto rolls or bread and serve immediately with condiments.

Serves 30.

WASABI MAYONNAISE

Wasabi is a spicy root vegetable used in Japanese cooking. You can usually find it in powdered form in small
tins at Asian or well-stocked general supermarkets. Be sure to keep this condiment in the cooler until just before serving.
Prepare it up to a week in advance and store in the refrigerator.

1 CUP MAYONNAISE

1 TEASPOON WASABI POWDER

Mix the two ingredients together and refrigerate up to 1 week.

LEMON CHICKEN BREASTS

Plan to marinate the chicken two days before the shower to allow flavors to penetrate the meat. You can prebake the breasts the day before. Finishing them on the grill at the party will take only a few minutes.

1 CUP OLIVE OIL, PLUS EXTRA TO
   BRUSH LEMON SLICES

1/2 CUP SHERRY VINEGAR

10 CLOVES GARLIC, CHOPPED

30 CHICKEN BREASTS, ON THE BONE

2 TABLESPOONS CRACKED PEPPER

10 LEMON HALVES

30 LEMON SLICES

Combine the oil, vinegar, and garlic. Pour over the chicken, sprinkle with the cracked pepper, and refrigerate overnight in an airtight container.

To bake, preheat oven to 350° F. Place the breasts on a baking sheet and bake for 30 minutes. Let cool slightly, then refrigerate until time to grill.

On a medium-hot grill, finish cooking chicken another 5 to 8 minutes per side, turning frequently. When done, remove to serving platter and squeeze juice from the lemon halves over the warm chicken. Brush the lemon slices with olive oil and grill quickly 1 to 2 minutes per side. Place one lemon slice atop each chicken breast and serve.

Serves 30.

BLACK BEAN AND ROASTED CORN SALAD

This quick-and-easy salad can be made with your favorite salsa recipe or a freshly prepared version from
a Mexican deli or the refrigerator section of your supermarket. Prepare the recipe up to two days in advance, and
keep refrigerated until ready to serve.

---

6 EARS FRESH CORN, SHUCKED AND
BOILED

4 CANS (14 OUNCES EACH) BLACK
BEANS, RINSED AND DRAINED

1 BUNCH GREEN ONIONS, THINLY
SLICED

1 BUNCH CILANTRO, STEMMED AND
ROUGHLY CHOPPED

16 OUNCES FRESH MILD SALSA

Place the cooked corn on a medium-hot grill or grill pan and cook a few minutes on all sides until slightly blackened. Remove from grill and set aside. When cool, cut the kernels from husk using a large knife and holding the husk perpendicular to the cutting surface. In a large bowl, combine the corn and the remaining ingredients, stirring and tossing to blend. Refrigerate until ready to serve, up to 2 days.

Serves 30.

This variation on a classic can be prepped the day before and assembled just before serving. Bocconcini are small balls of fresh mozzarella typically found at gourmet or Italian delis. If necessary, you can substitute larger fresh mozzarella balls cut into 1-inch chunks. If baby yellow tomatoes are not available, substitute cherry tomatoes.

1/2 CUP RED WINE VINEGAR OR
    BALSAMIC VINEGAR

2 TABLESPOONS DIJON MUSTARD

1 TABLESPOON SALT

1 TEASPOON PEPPER

3/4 CUP EXTRA VIRGIN OLIVE OIL

3 BASKETS CHERRY TOMATOES,
    HALVED

3 BASKETS BABY YELLOW PEAR
    TOMATOES, HALVED

FOUR 16-OUNCE CONTAINERS
    BOCCONCINI, DRAINED
    AND HALVED

2 CUPS FRESH BASIL LEAVES, LEFT
    WHOLE IF SMALL, OR ROUGHLY
    CHOPPED

SALT AND PEPPER

Combine the first four ingredients in a small bowl. Using a small wire whisk, slowly add the oil, whisking continuously. Store in a glass jar or airtight container. When ready to serve, combine the tomatoes, bocconcini, and basil and toss with the dressing. Season with salt and pepper.

Serves 30.

RUSTIC PEACH TART

At the height of summer, nothing is better than plump, juicy peaches and tangy raspberries, but you can substitute nearly any fruit in season. The tart can be served immediately or baked the day before the shower and refrigerated up to one day in its tin, wrapped in plastic. Keep it wrapped and in its tin for the trip to the beach.

For the crust:

1 1/2 CUPS ALL-PURPOSE FLOUR

2 TABLESPOONS SUGAR

1/4 TEASPOON SALT

1/2 CUP COLD UNSALTED BUTTER,
    CUT INTO PIECES

1 EGG YOLK

1/4 CUP ICE WATER

For the filling:

3/4 CUP ALMONDS

1/4 CUP SUGAR

3 OR 4 RIPE PEACHES, PITS REMOVED,
    THINLY SLICED

1/2 CUP PEACH PRESERVES

2 TABLESPOONS WATER

1 CUP FRESH RASPBERRIES

To make the crust, place the dry ingredients in a food processor and pulse several times to lightly blend. Add the butter pieces and pulse again until the mixture resembles a coarse meal. Add the egg yolk and pulse again to blend. Pour in the ice water through the shoot, a tablespoon at a time, until the dough is just holding together to form a ball. Gather dough into a ball and flatten to form an inch-thick round; wrap in plastic and refrigerate for 30 minutes.

On a lightly floured surface, roll the dough into a 10-inch round. Place dough in a 9-inch tart pan with removable bottom. Press dough into the bottom and up the sides of pan. Trim along the top to make a neat edge. Prick holes in bottom of crust with a fork and place in freezer for 1 hour.

Preheat oven to 375° F. To make the filling, place the almonds in food processor and pulse until coarsely ground. Add the sugar and pulse again until blended. Sprinkle the almond mixture evenly over bottom of tart crust. Arrange the peach slices on top, overlapping in concentric circles. Bake until pastry is golden, about 40 minutes.

While the tart is baking, heat the preserves with the water in a small saucepan over medium heat. Remove tart from oven and sprinkle the raspberries over the top. Strain preserves through a sieve over the warm tart and use a brush to distribute evenly.

Each tart serves 10.

CRAFT SUPPLIES AND ART PAPERS

Aahs
3223 Wilshire Boulevard
Santa Monica, CA 90403
(310) 829-1807
wrapping paper, boxes, tissue

Kate's Paperie
561 Broadway
New York, NY 10012
(212) 941-9816
papers, craft supplies, pens,
invitations, wrapping

Michael's Arts & Crafts
(972) 409-7660
call for store locations
craft supplies

Moskatel's
733 South San Julian Street
Los Angeles, CA 90014
(213) 689-4830
craft supplies

Paper Access
(800) PAPER-01
catalog available
papers, stationery, envelopes, tissue

Pearl Art Supply
(800) 451-7327
call for store locations
art and craft supplies

Soolip Paperie
8646 Melrose Avenue
West Hollywood, CA 90069
(310) 360-0545
stationery, papers, pens, envelopes, cards
printing service available

Standard Brands Party
3020 Wilshire Boulevard
Santa Monica, CA 90403
(310) 453-1094
party supplies, boxes, wrapping

Stats Floral Supply
120 South Raymond Avenue
Pasadena, CA 91105
(626) 795-9308
party supplies, craft supplies, silk flowers

FABRICS, NOTIONS, AND RIBBONS

B & J Fabrics
263 West 40th Street
New York, NY 10018
(212) 354-8150
fabrics

Bellocchio
8 Brady Street
San Francisco, CA 94103
(415) 864-4048
new and vintage ribbons

Britex Fabrics
146 Geary Street
San Francisco, CA 94108
(415) 392-2910
fabrics

Cinderella
60 West 38th Street
New York, NY 10018
(212) 840-0644
trimmings, ribbons, bridal accessories

F & S Fabrics
10629 West Pico Boulevard
Los Angeles, CA 90064
(310) 470-3398
fabrics, ribbons, trimmings, notions

Hyman Hendler & Sons
67 West 38th Street
New York, NY 10018
(212) 840-8393
new and vintage ribbons and trimmings

Lincoln Fabrics
1600 Lincoln Boulevard
Venice, CA 90291
(310) 396-5724
fabrics, ribbons, trimmings, some vintage

M & J Trimming
1008 Sixth Avenue
New York, NY 10018
(212) 391-9072
trimmings, buttons

Rosen & Chadick
246 West 40th Street
New York, NY 10018
(212) 869-0142
fabrics

Silk Trading Company
351 South La Brea Avenue
Los Angeles, CA 90036
(323) 954-9280
silk fabrics

Tinsel Trading
47 West 38th Street
New York, NY 10018
(212) 730-1030
new and vintage trimmings

HOUSEWARES AND FURNITURE

ABC Carpet & Home
888 Broadway
New York, NY 10003
(212) 473-3000
home accessories, furniture, linens, bath

Aero
132 Spring Street
New York, NY 10012
(212) 966-1500
furniture

Anthropologie
(800) 309-2500
www.anthropologie.com
tabletop, house accessories, linens

Banana Republic Home
(888) 906-2800
tabletop, linens

Bountiful
1335 Abbot Kinney Boulevard
Venice, CA 90291
(310) 450-3620
antique tableware, vases, linens

Calvin Klein Home
(800) 294-7978
tabletop, linens

Crate & Barrel
(800) 451-8217
tabletop, kitchenware

Fillamento
2185 Fillmore Street
San Francisco, CA 94115
(415) 931-2224
tabletop, house accessories, linens, bath

Garnet Hill
(800) 622-6216
catalog only
linens

Ikea
(800) 434-4532
www.ikea.com
tabletop, linens, kitchen

Kabuki
11355 Santa Monica Boulevard
West Los Angeles, CA 90025
(310) 477-2663
Japanese gifts and tableware

Maison Midi
150 South La Brea Avenue
Los Angeles, CA 90036
(323) 935-3154
tabletop, linens

Pom Pom
326 North La Brea Avenue
Los Angeles, CA 90036
(323) 934-2051
housewares, antiques, vintage linens and fabrics

Pottery Barn
(800) 588-6250
tabletop, linens, house accessories

Restoration Hardware
(800) 762-1005
tabletop, house accessories

Room with a View
1600 Montana Avenue
Santa Monica, CA 90403
(310) 998-5858
tabletop, linens

Shelter
7920 Beverly Boulevard
Los Angeles, CA 90048
(323) 937-3222
modern furniture

Sue Fisher King
3067 Sacramento Street
San Francisco, CA 94115
(415) 922-7276
tabletop, linens

Target
(800) 800-8800
call for store locations
housewares, party supplies

Troy
138 Greene Street
New York, NY 10013
(212) 941-4777
home accessories

Waterworks
(800) 998-2284
call for store locations
bath accessories, linens, toiletries

Wolfman Gold & Good Co.
117 Mercer Street
New York, NY 10012
(212) 431-1888
tabletop

Zona
97 Greene Street
New York, NY 10012
(212) 925-6750
home accessories, tabletop

KITCHENWARE AND BAKING SUPPLIES

Broadway Panhandler
477 Broome Street
New York, NY 10013
(212) 966-3434
gourmet kitchenware and baking supplies

Dean & Deluca
(800) 999-0306
*gourmet kitchenware, tabletop and
baking supplies*

NY Cake & Baking
56 West 22nd Street
New York, NY 10010
(212) 675-2253

Sur La Table
(800) 243-0852
call for store locations

Williams Sonoma
(800) 541-2233
call for store locations

FLOWERS/GARDENING

B & J Florists Supply
103 West 28th Street
New York, NY 10001
(212) 564-6086
floral supplies and craft

Bill's Flower Market
816 Sixth Avenue
New York, NY 10001
(212) 889-8154
floral supplies and craft

Hortus
284 East Orange Grove Boulevard
Pasadena, CA 91104
(626) 792-8255
gardening gifts, plants, flowers

Mellano & Company
766 Wall Street
Los Angeles, CA 90014
(213) 622-0796
fresh cut flowers and foliage

LINENS AND BEDDING

Koo Koo
512 Beatty Street
Vancouver, BC V6B 6GB
(604) 844-7445
towels, linens

Portico Home
72 Spring Street
New York, NY 10012
(212) 941-7800
linens, bath accessories

Tocca Casa
2123 Montana Avenue
Santa Monica, CA 90403
(310) 393-5593
bed linens

RENTALS

Absolute Party Rental
836 Ritchie Highway
Suite 19
Severna Park, MD 21146
(410) 544-7474

Arizona Tents & Events
1930 North 22nd Avenue
Phoenix, AZ 85009
(602) 252-8368

Classic Party Rentals
8476 Stellar Drive
Culver City, CA 90232
(310) 202-0011

Linen Lenders
14722 Oxnard
Van Nuys, CA 91411
(818) 781-1181